The Social Citizen

The Social Citizen:
Peer Networks and Political Behavior

Betsy Sinclair

The University of Chicago Press :: Chicago and London

Betsy Sinclair is assistant professor in the Department of Political Science at the University of Chicago.

The University of Chicago Press, Chicago 60637
The University of Chicago Press, Ltd., London
© 2012 by The University of Chicago
All rights reserved. Published 2012.
Printed in the United States of America

21 20 19 18 17 16 15 14 13 12   1 2 3 4 5

ISBN-13: 978-0-226-92281-2 (cloth)
ISBN-13: 978-0-226-92282-9 (paper)
ISBN-13: 978-0-226-92283-6 (e-book)
ISBN-10: 0-226-92281-2 (cloth)
ISBN-10: 0-226-92282-0 (paper)
ISBN-10: 0-26-92283-9 (e-book)

Library of Congress Cataloging-in-Publication Data
Sinclair, Betsy.
   The social citizen : peer networks and political behavior / Betsy Sinclair.
      pages.   cm. — (Chicago studies in American politics)
   ISBN-13: 978-0-226-92281-2 (cloth : alk. paper)
   ISBN-10: 0-226-92281-2 (cloth : alk. paper)
   ISBN-13: 978-0-226-92282-9 (pbk. : alk. paper)
   ISBN-10: 0-226-92282-0 (pbk. : alk. paper)
   [etc.]
   1. Political participation—United States.   2. Social networks—United States.   3. Voting—Social aspects—United States.   4. Social pressure.
I. Title.   II. Series: Chicago studies in American politics.
   JK1764.S542   2012
   306.20973—dc23   2012019396

To James & Brian

Contents

Acknowledgments

This book is the product of many conversations with advisors, colleagues, and friends. Mike Alvarez, Jonathan Katz, and Jonathan Nagler provided early mentorship on this project. Eric Oliver read numerous drafts, provided many comments, and had countless lunch meetings on how to write a book manuscript. Michael Dawson, John Brehm, John Padgett, John Balz, Jon Rogowski, Tom Wood, Jaira Harrington, Alex Bass, and Amir Fairdosi read various chapters. Jan Leighley helped me to focus on the central questions and innovations of the book. Lauren Blake provided research assistance for the chapter on campaign donations, and Margaret McConnell, Donald Green, and Melissa Michelson coauthored the field experiment research that informs the chapter on turnout. Jamie Druckman and James Fowler me helped ask the "big picture" questions. Will Howell encouraged me to keep writing. Ethan Bueno de Mesquita and the Harris School sponsored a conference on the book, which proved to be an invaluable academic experience, particularly by including Don Kinder, Bob Huckfeldt, Skip Lupia, and Jamie Druckman in the conversation. Kathryn Ciffolillo provided copyediting. Brian Rogers and the rest of the Sinclair family provided help, humor, grace, guidance and copyediting. James Rogers helped keep me to a deadline. I am thankful to them all.

Preface

People are inherently social. From fashion choices to moral standards, people continually adjust their behavior to fit in with those who surround them. Consequently, social relationships define our fundamental human experiences, from our sense of self to our preferences, and even affect our health. Reliance on a *social network*, the complex collection of relationships that arise from each person's geography, work, and leisure activities, is a common human characteristic. Most individuals have political networks embedded within their social networks. A *political network* consists of the social network members with whom an individual discusses politics, elections, or government. Political networks are part of the social component of human life.

But while people may be social, citizens are not, at least according to some of the most recognized models of political decision making. Indeed, most standard accounts—including those from a rational choice or psychological perspective—focus strictly on an individually based calculus, where each person independently, in isolation, chooses each political action. Citizens are assumed to make decisions free from the influence of their social network. When political scientists do recognize social influences, they usually consign them to the realm of mere information. In this view, our social networks shape our decisions to participate or our vote choices only insofar as they provide us with information that we may not already have; citizens, it would seem, are largely immune to social influence.

A growing body of empirical work challenges this portrayal by showing that the people with whom individuals interact affect a range of decisions including voting, protesting, and donating money (Christakis and Fowler 2009; Huckfeldt, Johnson, and Sprague 2004; Mutz 2006). Yet even this recent work leaves a number of fundamental questions unanswered: Do social networks really influence individuals, or do individuals choose networks with members who engage in similar behavior? If social networks matter, how do they work? Do they provide information, or is their function more basic and akin to peer pressure, causing mere mimicry or persuading people to conform to a set of social norms? Are there conditions or particular political activities that shape the impact of social influences? What are the implications of a social citizen for a well-functioning democracy?

The Social Citizen seeks to answer these questions by examining how our inherent sociability shapes our behavior as citizens. Utilizing a variety of experimental and survey data from settings as diverse as the wealthy suburbs of Illinois and the streets of South Los Angeles, this book identifies the social influences that underlie political activities ranging from voter turnout to political contributions. Its central finding is that people's social networks are not merely sources of information but have a direct and immediate influence on their political behavior. People's nonpolitical social connections often shape their actions as citizens. Because people form social bonds around a variety of common interests and because most people value these relationships and want to avoid disagreements, they often adopt the behavior of people in their social networks, even when this behavior conflicts with their own individual preferences. This book not only documents when such social influences occur but also examines what implications they have for the functioning of a democratic government.

The first chapter of the book provides a theoretical framework for the ensuing chapters, wherein a citizen resides within a social network, chosen based on shared characteristics. These characteristics are seldom political. When a network member, or a majority of network members, expresses an internalized social norm associated with a particular political behavior, the social citizen notices and conforms, particularly if the behavior is publicly visible. Each subsequent chapter introduces a different behavior and makes an argument for the presence of social network effects, where the social citizen has noticed peer behavior and conformed. These behaviors include two participation decisions, the decision to turn out to vote and the decision to donate to political campaigns and organizations, and two choices, the choice of candidate on the ballot and the choice of party identification. Cutting-edge methodological tools reveal that individuals are influenced by their social surroundings. By both resolving a number of methodological problems with selection effects, the role of information, and the limited availability of data and relaxing a number of statistical assumptions, these analyses allow more precise estimates of network effects than ever before. Social network effects are then tested with respect to the strength of social relationships, the extent to which the behavior is perceived to be a social norm, and the level of political sophistication of the individual.

Tying these chapters together is a consistent set of results that demonstrate that the social structure within which individuals interact predicts their political behavior and choices. Moving beyond correlations between political behavior and membership within particular groups, this research details how different political networks can produce starkly different outcomes. Current wisdom posits that networks affect individuals not through specific social influences but by providing information. The variety of techniques and data presented in this book permit some adjudication of these mechanisms. Individuals do not adapt because of information from their networks but because they face pressure to conform. These analyses suggest that social influence drives observed patterns of social network effects. If social influence results in increased conformity of expression and citizens do not form their preferences in isolation, then the realities of citizen political behavior do not accord with an idealized participatory democracy. This book explores four examples in which political behavior spreads via social relationships, described below.

Explicit social pressure results in voter turnout. Reporting the results of two field experiments, the second chapter evaluates mobilization strategies for leveraging the influence of social networks on voter turnout. The first experiment assesses the indirect mobilization effects of individuals within the voter's household and neighborhood. The second experiment focuses on the effects of mobilization by different types of canvassers: strangers and neighbors. Local, neighborhood-based canvassers armed with a mobilization message stimulate additional voter turnout, whereas strangers are not particularly effective. Both experiments find that individuals follow their network when behavioral norms are explicitly communicated but not when they are simply observed or when information about voting is communicated. Individuals are directly motivated to vote by social influence.

Political campaign donations pose the classic collective action problem: it is costly to participate and difficult, once enough other individuals participate, to maintain participation. The third chapter analyzes data from all federally recorded political contributions in the Illinois Tenth Congressional District. The amount of money donated is a function of the level of public visibility of individual giving. Giving is also tied to particular social relationships with friends and family. These patterns of giving suggest a social component in donation behavior. In-person interviews with the donors confirm these findings, specifically that individuals are regularly asked by their friends to pull out their checkbooks.

Why would a Democrat vote for a Republican candidate? Candidate choice is typically framed in terms of individual actors comparing the difference between the candidates' platform positions and their own individual preferences and then choosing the candidate who maximizes their individual expected utility. The fourth chapter incorporates the role of an individual's social relationships into that calculus using individual-level survey data that include an individual's self-identification of social context. Survey respondents completed a standard social network battery, and these responses measure voters' political networks in both the 2000 American National Election Studies (ANES) and the 2008 Cooperative Campaign Analysis Project. Once demographic and socioeconomic characteristics are controlled for, the results demonstrate that voters' social contexts partially determine individual candidate choices. Respondents change their preferences for particular candidates during the course of the campaign, and their preferences converge with those of their social networks.

Social relationships can sway the hearts and minds of partisans. Why would an individual report having a different party identification in November 2006 than in November 2004? Survey responses show that social relationships affect party identification; that is, respondents are more likely both to share partisanship with their social network and to converge toward the partisanship of those individuals over time. Using two distinct data sets from November 2006—the ANES pilot study and the Cooperative Congressional Election Study—chapter 5 shows that party identification has a social component. This extends earlier work in political science on the parent-child socialization of party identification with the finding that party identification will move toward the preferences of the social network over time, and the effect is particularly strong for close relationships.

These four substantive chapters collectively demonstrate that social relationships form around common characteristics but are not explicitly rooted in individual political preferences or behaviors. Democrats may form friendships with Republicans in the course of school PTA meetings, young nonvoters may form relationships with older voters in work environments, and neighbors can form friendships regardless of whether they contributed to the local congressional candidate's campaign. Because of the high value individuals place on these social relationships and the difficulty in sustaining relationships when disagreements occur, individual political preferences and behaviors compete with the desire for stable social relationships. Social influence, via direct and indirect social pressure, determines individuals' political preferences and behaviors, whereby they compare themselves to each member of their social network and adopt the politics and behaviors most supported by those in their network. This social phenomenon challenges the current wisdom that individuals rely on these relationships solely for political information in order to make independent decisions. Citizens do not make political decisions in isolation from one another.

Social influence complicates the democratic process, as an ideal democracy relies on individual political expression and preferences. To the extent that people's relationships influence their politics, social networks drive behavioral patterns that dictate the quality of representation in a democracy. Democracy is defined by responsiveness to participatory citizens. In an ideal democracy, citizens have equal opportunities to form their preferences and to express those preferences with weight equal to the preferences of others (Dahl 1989). Yet this work suggests that any true democracy is composed of social citizens, and particular democratic outcomes are driven by particular social structures. Participation decisions are influenced by individuals who exert social pressure to maintain the social order of a participatory democracy (Garfinkel 1984). While these social networks are incredibly precarious, they shape the processes by which a participatory democracy functions and is sustained.

Who is a social citizen? A *social citizen* is an individual whose social networks intertwine with her political preferences and behaviors. Some citizens are more likely to be susceptible to social influence, and some behaviors are more likely to be contagious. As the empirical chapters demonstrate, if social pressure is the mechanism that dictates social influence, then there will be particular kinds of individuals whom we can identify as social. These citizens are the product of their social environment. They reflect the political norms of their social networks and not their own individual preferences, in stark contrast to the citizens of an idealized democracy.

Yet social citizens play a key role in civil society. Social citizens have the potential to transform their political environment. If the diffusion of political behavior via particular social structures can be considered epidemic, then one individual—a social citizen—can have significant impact in maintaining particular political norms, such as sustaining voter turnout. The contagion is limited, as not every social relationship results in diffusion of behavior—only those that are immediately socially proximate. However, by influencing her peers in her social network, a social citizen has the potential to exert indirect influence on individuals outside of the immediate social network. The actions of the social citizen can affect individuals she has never met. Our democracy is based not on individual participation but on collective participation. Political networks are key factors in understanding political behavior, and the foundations of participatory democracy are based in social communication between social citizens.

1

Introduction: Social Pressure and Participatory Democracy

What motivates a nonvoter to participate in politics? Why do some individuals donate so much money to political candidates and organizations? What motivates a registered Democrat to vote for a Republican candidate? Why would a college student choose to register for the Republican Party when the rest of her family are registered Democratic? This book addresses these questions with the larger goal of identifying what may be the most critical determinant of political behavior. Specifically, in contrast to common portrayals of political actors as atomistic, citizens' political actions depend largely on their social interactions. Making sense of citizens' political decisions requires a sustained understanding of their social networks.

Politics are incredibly contagious in social networks. Shared political behaviors of an individual's social network affect both participation and political choices. When friends and family talk about politics, they are referring to tightly held personal norms of civic behavior, and in close personal relations it is difficult to disagree about such beliefs. As Michael MacKuen (1990, 94) notes, "Politics probably incorporates more of a sense of morality than many other topics of conversation." Perhaps, then, people are cautious to whom they talk about politics (Eliasoph 1998). Yet voters do talk to their families and friends about politics regularly. In the 2004 American National Election Studies (ANES), 80 percent of the respondents reported having conversations with their families and friends about politics.[1]

What are these friends talking about? Do these social interactions matter? There are good reasons to think not. Indeed, these friends are unlikely to be sharing information. One of the most notable features of democratic citizens is their lack of political knowledge. An extensive literature documents the lack of political interest, information, or sophistication among most citizens. Voters may not know the number of senators from their state, for example, and, less surprisingly, may have difficulty locating themselves and the candidates on an ideological spectrum, remembering the names of candidates, or knowing where any particular candidate stands on a broad set of issues (Almond and Verba 1963; Berelson, Lazarsfeld, and McPhee 1954; Campbell et al. 1960; Converse 1964; Kinder and Sears 1985). Voters are often reported to be poorly informed about the candidates' positions (Campbell et al. 1960; Palfrey and Poole 1987; Alvarez 1998). Given this ostensible disengagement, is it plausible that social interactions play a pivotal role in shaping political attitudes and behaviors? Political conversations need not be particularly informative to have an effect: it need not be information transmission that drives the impact of social groups.

Instead, individuals are likely to be talking about politics in the context of constructing a social and political identity. There are two possibilities whereby individuals are influenced by their social environment via explicitly external channels.[2] First, as discussed above, some individuals are persuaded by information, shared between their social ties, to change their political behavior. In this instance, political persuasion occurs as a consequence of explicit social communication. Persuasion, some argue, occurs as a consequence of deliberation or exposure to particular rhetoric. The second channel is that of conformity to a social norm for purely social purposes. In this case, individuals mirror the political norms of those within their social network who have strong normative preferences to particular political behaviors, like voting or donating to campaigns. This last channel can help to simply maintain a pattern of behavior. This is distinct from compliance, where an individual adopts a particular behavior based upon the coercive power of the social network. In this last channel, individuals adopt norms they believe are correct as well as socially desirable for their social ties. It is not necessary for one individual to directly request compliance from another individual, although personal requests are possible. It is sufficient for one individual to observe the behavior of another through regular social interactions: this kind of interaction facilitates social learning about political norms.

This chapter proceeds by characterizing an individual's political network. Political networks may influence an individual's politics via two primary mechanisms—information and social pressure—and the section that follows distinguishes these two mechanisms and the kinds of empirical patterns that emerge from each one. The remainder of the book is then outlined in the following sections, with particular attention to its methodological contributions and the diversity of approaches for identifying political networks.

A Political Network

Citizens' *social networks* describe the collection of individuals tied to them by social connections, such as friendships, family relationships, or work colleagues. Each individual's social network forms by some combination of choice, where the individual purposefully selects network members, and chance, where the individual randomly forms relationships with others. A *political network* consists of a subset of these social peers with whom an individual discusses politics, elections, or government. Political networks overlay preexisting social networks; they are not necessarily geographically based but are founded on strong social relationships, likely dominated by primary group members with whom the individual communicates about external social norms.

Throughout this book, different techniques are presented to establish an individual's political network. Unless the individual has been solicited to identify specific individuals with whom she has political interactions, however, the collection of relationships presented encompass her larger social network. Insight into what the larger social network structure looks like can be drawn from sociology and microeconomics, where a significant amount of work has been done to describe the formulation of social networks. In this literature, individuals are described as nodes in a graph where links (either directed or not) represent connections between people (friendships, coauthors, or simply people who know each other). Examples of social networks abound: a favorite game for movie lovers, Six Degrees of Kevin Bacon; the social networking website Facebook; and Milgram's (1967) classic study of "small worlds," in which he examined how many times a letter was handled before it was received by the intended recipient. The shape of the social network is determined by where links are formed, their distribution, and their density. Political networks are subsets of social networks that are composed of links formed both randomly and by individuals searching for other individuals.[3] Individuals tend to have political networks with low density—that is, in very few cases are the political discussion partners of one individual socially connected to each other—and to be asymmetric: an individual may identify someone as a political discussant, but she may not necessarily reciprocate (Huckfeldt and Sprague 1995; Huckfeldt, Johnson, and Sprague 2004).

Numerous empirical studies have identified the presence of political networks, and a number of national probability sample surveys have incorporated items designed to document their presence.[4] The 2000 ANES social network battery offered insight into the interaction of disagreement and social ties (Huckfeldt, Johnson, and Sprague 2004). This study clarified that political networks tend not to be very large. In the 2000 ANES, only 18 percent of the survey respondents could name four individuals with whom they discuss politics. Over 40 percent of the discussants were relatives of the respondent, 25 percent were coworkers, 10 percent attended the same church, and 20 percent were neighbors. The average respondent reported speaking to each discussant a couple of times per week.

Huckfeldt and Sprague (1995) asked respondents specifically about their political contacts and then interviewed the contacts to get a more complete understanding of an individual's network. They examined both the 1984 and 1996 presidential elections looking for the existence and effects of political networks. In examining the 1984 presidential election they focused on the effects of an individual's preferences (and the distribution of preferences) on the choice of "political discussion partners."[5] Their survey asked respondents whom they cast their votes for and how they believed their discussion partners cast their votes. Their results indicate that individuals are more likely to have conversations with people who agree with them but that there is some amount of political heterogeneity. They found that two-thirds of Reagan voters had discussants who reported voting for Reagan and that 57 percent of Mondale voters had discussants who reported voting for Mondale.[6] Political networks are generally homogeneous in terms of socioeconomic and demographic characteristics but are not completely characterized by political homogeneity. Political networks can form as an unintended consequence of social groups or for actual political purposes.

The observed correlation between the survey respondents' and their discussants' choices in the Huckfeldt and Sprague Reagan-Mondale results is likely to be present within most political networks. This correlation could be attributable to a history of political conversations with some of their network members in each election cycle, for example, or could be attributable to the selection of politically similar network members. This type of correlation makes it particularly difficult to identify network effects. This book employs a range of empirical strategies to circumvent the identification problems generated by this kind of correlation, such as taking advantage of changing preferences over time or intervening with a randomized field experiment. These empirical strategies are discussed further in the chapters that follow.

Why is there such a desire to mirror the political norms of the social network? Social scientists have long understood that most individuals have a fundamental need to belong to and affiliate with groups (Baumeister and Leary 1995).[7] Yet it has never been theorized that the individual conforms with the group on all issues; rather, individuals are selectively pressured on those issues that are essential to the stability of the group (Steiner 1954; Walsh 2004). Disagreement with respect to social-political norms can undermine the stability of the group. Individuals are likely to have their own preferences about politics, but as elections and politics become socially visible during an election campaign, individuals feel pressure to conform to the norms of their social networks (Berelson, Lazarsfeld, and McPhee 1954; Huckfeldt and Sprague 1995). In the context of casual conversations, individuals are likely to become aware of political differences between themselves and other members of their social network.[8] To this extent, then, there is a range of topics for which social conformity is likely to exist. Political behavior, particularly related to social norms, is likely to fall into this category periodically, particularly preceding an election. That is, groups succeed at collectively establishing political norms when politics become a salient component of the group conversation (Merei 1952; Katz and Lazarsfeld 1955; Walsh 2004). This happens as a consequence of the desire to establish a common social identity (Conover et al. 2002). Individuals face pressures to conform (Festinger 1954), and responding to these pressures leads to shared political behavior. An individual will balance her personal preferences and choices against those of her social context, and most individuals prefer to agree with their social network than to defend their individual politics. Thus individuals succumb to social pressure and adopt the political preferences and behaviors of their social network.

That individuals prefer to belong to groups with homogeneous preferences is clear from their selection of a social network. These choices are governed not by political preferences, however, but by social prefer-

ences. Individuals choose their social networks based on shared characteristics such as socioeconomic and demographic characteristics. Political characteristics are likely to be correlated to these variables and thus
are also likely to be shared (Lazar et al. 2008). Lazarsfeld, Berelson,
and Gaudet (1948, 137) write, "Most people interacted during the campaign with others with shared social characteristics, shared attitudes
and, thus, shared political pre-dispositions." Yet individuals primarily
form social relationships based on shared nonpolitical characteristics.
Weatherford (1982, 129) finds that the variables that affect the degree of
social interaction between local residents "do not contribute to network
politicization."[9] Even groups in which politics are regularly discussed
are not formed based on shared political preferences (Walsh 2004).

The phenomenon of individuals preferring groups with homogeneous
preferences is referred to as homophily: the tendency of an individual
to associate with similar others (Lazarsfeld and Merton 1954; Coleman
1958; McPherson, Smith-Lovin, and Cook 2001). Homophily is most
likely to occur among those of the same race and ethnicity, age, religion,
education, occupation, and gender, roughly in that order (McPherson,
Smith-Lovin, and Cook 2001). Social relationships, despite homophily with respect to socioeconomic and demographic characteristics,
are unlikely to be characterized by complete political homogeneity, as
political issues do not dominate interpersonal conversation or interest.
Interest in politics is mainly focused on election cycles, and there is consistent evidence that individuals do disagree about their politics in the
course of elections (Huckfeldt and Sprague 1995; Huckfeldt et al. 1995;
Huckfeldt, Sprague, and Levine 2000; Huckfeldt, Johnson, and Sprague
2004; Ikeda and Huckfeldt 2001; Schmitt-Beck 2003). Social networks
are established, then, both by choice and by circumstance (Jackson and
Rogers 2007; Mollenhorst, Volker, and Flap 2008), and relationships
change frequently. Approximately half of all close relationships change
every seven years. Assuming the presence of new ties, upon which no
political pressure has been exerted outside of an election cycle, there will
be disagreement within the group regarding politics during the course
of an election (Mollenhorst, Volker, and Flap 2007, 2008).

To summarize, a basic theory of human sociability explains the instances when we make collective choices or engage in collective behavior. Individuals choose homogeneous social networks. Particularly during election cycles or at other times when politics is likely to be salient
in casual conversations, a political network overlays each individual's
social connections. The political network is not homogeneous because
it is not formed based on political preferences but rather on other social

preferences. Citizens' political attitudes and behavior depend critically on social groups. These groups form for nonpolitical purposes, but the norms of group behavior, at critical times, lead to what otherwise appear to be surprising political actions, such as when a registered Democrat votes for a Republican candidate. Yet social networks will only influence individuals if network members give voice to a particular political norm, sincerely adhering to the political norm in an observable way. In this sense, human sociability shapes democratic outcomes. Put simply, individuals do not want to disappoint their friends and family, and this is how politics are contagious. Not only is human sociability important for understanding the origins of political behaviors, but it also raises serious questions about how democracies work, since the contagion process may not stem from political preferences but from social pressures resulting from the nonpolitical dynamics of network formation.

Information or Social Pressure

While some of the existing literature has documented the influence of political networks, they are seldom seen as a dominant explanation for political behavior, in large part because of the difficulty of identifying the mechanism that drives the observed correlations in behavior between network members. Linking the existing research on the influence of social networks to new research on four political behaviors (voting, donating, choosing a candidate, and choosing a party identification) reveals patterns that attribute a component of political behavior to social pressure exerted by a political network. Individuals are embedded in particular political networks, and their networks are a component of their decision calculus. The network preferences determine, to some extent, individual participation and choices. The type of network—whether it is one in which individuals regularly interact, for example, or whether the network is primary or secondary—determines the amount of network influence. Particular behaviors are also more or less likely to be exposed to network effects.

There are two principal theories regarding how individuals might adopt the behaviors of their political network. First, individuals may rely on their social networks for information, in particular from trusted sources. Social networks may provide arguments to use for deliberation, may provide information about candidate platforms or places where donations are needed, or may simply relay how and when to cast a ballot. Information has typically been considered contagious across political networks; this is the most common explanation for the presence of social network effects (Sokhey and McClurg 2008; Djupe and Sokhey 2011). Second, individuals may face social pressure from their political networks. Individuals rely on their social networks to maintain their social identity and may base their preferences on social comparison with their network. In this case, the network exerts social pressure on each member, particularly if a majority of network members have homogeneous preferences regarding a political or social norm. There are strong arguments underpinning each of these theories, and each theory generates a distinct set of hypotheses regarding a set of empirical regularities. For example, if social pressure dominates a citizen's experience of democracy, then across behaviors there should be a network effect. The effect should be determined more by intimate network ties and less by a broader social context or other indirect influences. This effect should be larger for relationships in which there is a tighter social connection. In contrast, network influence generated by shared information should not vary based on the social proximity of the relationship.

Information. Suppose that a voter determines which candidate to support in an upcoming election. How could information from her political network influence her choice? Voters' information about candidates comes from many sources before an election, some trustworthy and some not. Voters know that campaigns attempt to influence voter opinions by producing biased information, but they also know that more objective sources exist. Not all of this information is free, however. While campaigns may spend millions of dollars to bring information into voters' living rooms, voters must actively seek out objective sources. While voters may realize that they receive heavily biased information from the campaign, they may not have the interest or time to investigate unbiased sources and procure information. There is, however, a compromise between spending time and effort reading about candidates and simply viewing campaign advertising. It is possible to rely on a trusted source, specifically someone who has procured enough information to make an informed decision and will not relay heavily biased information (Downs 1957). If there is no single individual who is willing to pay the cost to procure all the information about the candidates, it is also possible for individuals to aggregate information (McKelvey and Ordeshook 1985a, 1985b, 1990; Converse 1962). This aggregation process occurs completely naturally through friendships (Huckfeldt, Johnson, and Sprague 2004).

If political information can be aggregated through a network of friends, then no single individual need spend much time researching candidate positions. A large literature exists about how voters take cues from sources around them to minimize the costs of determining which candidate to support (Conover and Feldman 1989; Hamilton 1981; Higgins and King 1981; Miller et al. 1976; Kinder 1978). Downs (1957) formalized this concept of taking cues from a trustworthy source; Lupia and McCubbins (1998) extend this idea to include endorsements of interest groups. Voters can be overwhelmed with the range of information available to them, and the process of filtering to obtain unbiased information is difficult when one is faced with biased media sources or political advertisements. Instead, voters look to the people they can trust to help them make choices. These people are often neighbors, friends, and family members—people with whom the voter has a preexisting relationship. These individuals may be thought of as local opinion leaders—individuals who have particular expertise in the area of politics (Huckfeldt 2001; Huckfeldt et al. 1998). It is not very costly to have conversations with friends, and it takes only a little time. When a voter gains information through conversations, she need not spend hours researching the candidates to gather enough information to make an informed choice. Instead, the voter may aggregate the information she receives in the course of conversation. Thus political information may be transmitted via a social network.

When a voter aggregates information from friends and family, the conclusions she can draw are constrained by the information available within her social framework. Then, regardless of the voter's preferences, she is likely to have the same beliefs about politics as her friends and family. Suppose also that the voter is likely to have similar ideological preferences as her friends and family, because of homophily in her social network. Thus it is likely that since her beliefs are correlated with those around her, she will choose the same candidate, donate to the same campaigns, register for the same party, and turn out to cast a ballot in the same elections as those in her social network, both because of similarity of preferences and because of shared information. Since some social ties, especially those within families, tend to be fairly constant, it is unlikely that we will observe large changes in participation or choice patterns because of social network changes. This explanation is consistent with the findings of Campbell et al. (1960) that people rely heavily on their party identification predispositions and with those of Jennings and Niemi (1981) that children tend to inherit their parents' party identification. Party identification powerfully predicts vote choice. Furthermore, aggregation of political information can produce voting patterns in which voters' choices for candidates resemble the voting choices of those around them. If the theoretical framework is borne out by empirical evidence, then voters who are less sophisticated or have less information should be more likely to be affected by their political networks.

An extension of the role of network information is that political opinions arise from the aggregation of deliberative arguments within a social network. This requires a different kind of information to be transmitted between network members. This theoretical framework is argued by Mutz (2006), who presents comparative statistics regarding the exposure of individuals to "rationales" for their perspective and their political preferences and describes how individuals are exposed to political agreement and disagreement. There are particular requirements for deliberation to occur: it should take place in small groups, it should involve the open exchange of viewpoints, and all participants should have equal status (Mendelberg 2002). Political discussion networks may meet these criteria. True deliberation requires high-quality communication (Rawls 1993), and deliberative disagreement may result in a decrease in political participation or political discussion (MacKuen 1990; Mutz and Martin 2001; Mutz 2002a, 2002b, 2006). If empirical work reveals that deliberation is the mechanism that drives social network effects, then individuals who are less sophisticated or have less information should be more likely to be affected by their social networks. These individuals should also, if exposed to disagreement, be likely to stop participating in the political process. Additionally, in this case, it is the message that has the potential to persuade, not the messenger. That is, there should be no heterogeneous effects based on the intensity of the personal relationship between the individual and her network members.

Social Pressure. Information may not solely determine the influence that networks exert on individual political behavior. Social pressure is another possible influence. Political scientists have long been interested in how people form political opinions. Lazarsfeld, Berelson, and Gaudet (1948) concluded that campaigns were not the catalyst for opinion shifts. They determined that community opinion leaders played key roles in individual political decisions. Campbell et al. (1960) looked down the funnel of causality: party identification was the most crucial component in determining vote choice, and a sizable literature describes the formation of party identification as a product of parental ideology (Jennings and Niemi 1981; Franklin 1984; Achen 2002). Inheriting party identification is one example of how social relationships may influence voting behavior. The changing nature of social relationships may also explain how individuals change their opinions (Abramowitz and Sanders 1998).

Individuals conform to the social norms of their networks. Existing literature on social network effects evaluates the extent to which an individual's nonpolitical behavior is determined by the behaviors and choices of her social networks. Happiness, for example, and health have large network effects (Fowler and Christakis 2008a, 2008b). These studies have typically found that behaviors such as smoking (Christakis and Fowler 2008), obesity (Christakis and Fowler 2007, 2008), and educational attainment (Zimmer and Toma 1999; Hoxby 2000) are contagious across social ties and unrestricted by geography. Furthermore, and key to the theory of social pressure, while these behaviors appear to be contagious within networks, they do not appear to be broadly affected by the general information available in society at large. That is, people imitate *only* their network members. As Christakis and Fowler (2009, 115) indicate with respect to the spread of obesity, this "illustrates the difference between ideology and norms. People see images of ideal body types in the media, but they are less influenced by such images—by this ideology—than they are by the actions and the appearance of the very real people to whom they are actually connected." Imitation of networks with respect to nonpolitical behavior is "deeply rooted in our biological capacity for empathy and even morality, and it is connected to our origins as a social species" (Christakis and Fowler 2009, 112). Political behaviors are also likely to be socially contagious. Nickerson (2008) and Green, Gerber, and Larimer (2008) have argued that the decision to turn out to cast a ballot, for example, is motivated by social pressure and is socially contagious.

Academic research has argued that individuals are strongly motivated to conform. Psychological experiments, including the famous Asch experiments in which individuals misidentify the shortest line in order to agree with their peers (Asch 1955, 1956, 1963; Ross, Bierbrauer, and Hoffman 1976), have demonstrated the potential power of social conformity. Indeed, individuals are willing to engage in altruistic punishment to enforce social norms, suggesting that conformity is ingrained in our basic nature (Fowler, Johnson, and Smirnov 2005; Fowler 2005a). Additionally, individuals appear to be strongly motivated by egalitarianism (Dawes et al. 2007). Social pressure requires only that an individual listen to a network peer more than to strangers. There does not necessarily need to be punishment for nonconformity for social pressure to occur. Indeed, the research presented in this book does not resolve whether or not individuals are punished for not conforming. Mutz's (2006) finding that individuals are less likely to participate if continuously exposed to disagreement suggests, however, that there may be a punishment component for nonconformity. That individuals tend to "praise those who uphold norms and scorn those who violate them" may be sufficient motivation for individuals to monitor the norms held by their political networks, regardless of whether they expect to be punished for not conforming (Bolsen 2010, 6).

Responding to social pressure confirms a perceived obligation to conform to the behavior of the social network. For this to occur, network members must express a social norm. It requires an audience—that is, the behavior must be observed in some way, and pressure must be exerted, even if subtly. That is, members of the network must express their desire for others to adhere to the social norm. Work in social psychology has demonstrated that social pressure can induce compliance that is supported by social norms (Cialdini and Goldstein 2004; Cialdini and Trost 1998; Scheff 2000). The Grameen Bank attributes its high levels of microloan repayment to social pressure (Yunus 2003). Green, Gerber, and Larimer (2008) attribute to social pressure the increased turnout for elections when each voter receives a postcard indicating that each turnout decision is a matter of public record. Individuals who are exposed to higher levels of political conversation within their networks—that is, are exposed to more political norms—are more likely to participate in politics (Knoke 1990; Leighley 1990; Kenny 1992; Lake and Huckfeldt 1998; McClurg 2003; Klofstad 2007). Individuals appear to be highly sensitive to even small amounts of social pressure. Perhaps, then, the political network exerts social pressure on each individual, resulting in a correlation in political behavior between the individual and the network.

Distinguishing between the Two Mechanisms. Which kinds of political behavior will be most susceptible to social pressure? Individuals are more susceptible to social pressure when behavior is publicly visible and when the level of friends' supervision is high. Geographically proximate network ties should produce greater effects. Greater effects should also reflect the intensity of the relationship (e.g., individuals are more influenced by family than by friends and by those with whom they have more frequent conversations than by those with whom they converse less). More intense relationships are more likely to confer a sense of identity and value on the individual (Harmon-Jones et al. 1996). If the effects are purely social, then there should not be heterogeneous effects based on the individual's level of education—that is, the individual should not experience greater or lesser effects based upon their need for information. Varying the messenger—whether a neighbor or a stranger delivers the same information—should not determine the degree of influence if social network influence is determined by shared information. Yet if social network influence is determined by social pressure, the neighbor should have a greater effect than the stranger.

Candidate choice and party identification are subject to very different network effects. The decision to choose a party repeats each election cycle—and thus is continuously exposed to the same network pressures from family relationships. The choice of candidate is made each election cycle. We should observe more stability in the network pressures for party identification than for candidate choice, as communication about the social norms of the group with respect to party choice happens more frequently than communication about candidate choice. Political moderates should be more susceptible to social pressure, because the costs of deferring to the preferences of the network are lower than for individuals who have strong personal preferences.

Turnout and campaign giving are much more publicly visible, as both are matters of public record. Additionally, both behaviors may occur in front of others; the act of casting a ballot at a local polling place and the act of attending a fundraiser may easily be observed by other network members. Thus these are effects that should be driven by social norms.

Networked Democracy: Participation and Choice

Participatory democracy consists of two distinct actions by citizens: the decision to participate and the choice of elected representatives (Dahl 1971). At a minimum, the decision to participate consists of casting a ballot, but there are many other ways in which a citizen can participate in the democratic process—by writing to her representatives, for example. In the United States, citizens fund campaigns, and thus for many individuals, participation also includes financial support of particular candidates. Citizens must choose among available candidates and express individual preferences by casting a ballot and are often required to provide their party identification when registering to vote. Participatory democracy places an enormous number of demands on its citizens.

Our political system relies on the sincere expression of individuals who belong to social networks. In an ideal democracy, individuals have equal opportunity to form their preferences and to express them in equal weight with others. In a networked democracy, individuals influence each other and collectively establish norms of political behavior. A democracy that results from citizens being influenced by each other is very different than the one Dahl (1989) imagined. In *The American Voter*, Campbell et al. (1960) limited their focus to individual behavior for political causes. Yet most of life does not involve politics but revolves around social interactions. How do these social interactions—many of which are driven by nonpolitical incentives—influence political behaviors?

Much of political science studies citizens as isolated survey cases and theorizes about them as individual rational actors. Traditional models of political science have construed political decisions as being produced by individual actors. Citizens are typically seen in isolation from each other. They reason, carefully form opinions, and express those opinions. Beginning with the 1940 Eric County study, Lazarsfeld, Berelson, and Gaudet (1948) noticed that socioeconomic status was the best predictor of people's voting decisions. Other scholars have argued that the value of participating is expressive and not driven by any type of individual payoff-maximizing calculus (Schuessler 2000). Little work has argued that an individual's choices are constrained by her social network preferences. Yet the existing literature is suggestive of these constraints. While candidate choices are typically defined by ideological preferences, party identification is often framed as relying on family relationships. The decision to cast a ballot has long been considered a function of cost, ideology, pivotality, and civic duty, but the act of voting is difficult to reconcile with this calculus (Downs 1957; Riker and Ordeshook 1968; Green and Shapiro 1994). Recent advances have begun to consider a social component in the decision calculus, operationalized by a civic duty term. That is, individuals participate in accordance with social norms. Rolfe (2012) argues that voters' decisions are conditional on their social networks and that turnout is consistent with a model of voters navigating their social interactions. Moreover, while political participation appears to be affected by cost, as participation is a function of income and race, one way in which costs can decrease is via the participation of individuals' neighbors, as documented by Verba, Schlozman, and Brady (1995).

Implicit motivations for both participation and choices have resulted in a number of paradoxes and are insufficient to generate predictions consistent with the magnitudes of participation observed in the world. Donating money to candidates and other kinds of campaigns is difficult to reconcile with a model built on an atomistic, rational actor. In particular, individual models of campaign donations suffer from collective action problems (Olson 1965; Oliver and Marwell 1988). Explicit motivations based upon social networks offer a likely opportunity to understand political behavior.

Each of the four chapters that follow identifies social network effects in one aspect of political behavior—either a choice or a participation decision. Each chapter differs from the main models in American politics by privileging social network effects. The goal of each chapter is twofold: first, to contribute to the identification of social network effects with respect to that behavior, via either new data or a new methodology, and second, to identify the mechanism that drives the social network effect. The findings reveal evidence of social pressure. The study of political behavior is populated by theoretical models and empirical measurements of individual-level decisions made in isolation. In this framework, individuals may incorporate the preferences of others into their strategic considerations but never into their own personal preferences. Yet individuals do not make their political decisions in isolation. Instead, individuals bring a social foundation to their political choices and participation decisions. An individual's social network plays a key role in determining her political behavior.

Existing scholarship has documented the presence of network effects for a number of political behaviors but has not documented the mechanism that drives these effects or determined that the relationship is causal. By looking for patterns of effects across behaviors and identification strategies, it is possible to understand the network effect on an individual and that each citizen's behavior is a product of a social environment. It is possible to unravel the mechanism that drives social network effects.

The Problems of Homophily and Locating Political Networks

This book illustrates the effects of political networks via four distinct topics. Chapter 2 establishes network effects for voter turnout, where individuals are more likely to cast a ballot when the request to do so originates from a social network member. Chapter 3 finds that family, friends, and neighbors are able to elicit campaign donations. Chapter 4 reveals that political networks influence individuals' choices of candidates, and chapter 5 shows that political networks influence individuals' choices of party identification. Each chapter resolves the problem of homophily and identifies the political network differently. The range of empirical strategies for addressing homophily and identifying networks, combined with a common finding that these networks influence an individual's politics, support the book's primary claim that networks are influential in political behavior.

Homophily. One of the key concerns in establishing the influence of a political network on a particular network member is *homophily*, the tendency of an individual to associate with similar others (Lazarsfeld and Merton 1954; Coleman 1958; McPherson, Smith-Lovin, and Cook 2001). Since individuals choose network members who are similar to themselves, in empirical work, particular strategies are necessary to avoid overstating the influence of the network on the individual (Aral, Muchnik, and Sundararajan 2009). In the analyses that follow, three such empirical strategies substantiate that networks indeed influence their members. First, a set of randomized field experiments allow for the introduction of a mobilization stimulus to track through a social network, defined by geographic proximity to the member. Randomization solves one aspect of the selection problem attributable to homophily. By comparing a set of individuals (and their network members) who do not receive the stimulus to those who do, it is possible not only to observe the direct effect of the network but also to determine to what extent the stimulus is spread within each network. Second, panel data on political networks are reported in chapters 4 and 5, and it is possible to see each individual's political preferences converging with those of the network members over time. These two strategies provide clear causal evidence of the presence of network effects while avoiding the perils of causal estimation in the face of homophily. The third strategy is to control for the social characteristics that generate homophily. This is done in all four substantive chapters. These three strategies do not completely solve the selection problem, but they advance our knowledge about the ways in which social networks influence individual politics.

High levels of homophily also demonstrate something important about how politics are communicated. Individuals clearly do not like to disagree with their social network—this is demonstrated by the fact that their networks are so highly homogeneous. This suggests many individuals have already anticipated the costs of disagreement and have devised particular strategies to avoid disagreement. Further, across analyses, it appears that closer personal relationships exert greater social influence. That is, if the network were instead *randomly* assigned, there should be almost no influence. Politics are only contagious within networks that are characterized by homophily. While this complicates any estimation strategy, it illustrates the way in which political behavior is maintained by a set of personal norms. Individuals do not follow the behavior of strangers or society at large. They follow the behavior of their friends and family.

Locating Networks. Political networks are typically difficult to measure. Who are the political network members? How do we identify them? There are three basic strategies to locate each individual's political network. First, one may assume that all the network members are contained in a particular geography. Second, one may assume that all network members are exposed by some shared behavioral action. Third, one may simply ask individuals to identify the members of their network. Each of these approaches measures a different aspect of a political network. By incorporating different measurement strategies, it is possible to understand the key components of an individual's network and to consider the impact of an individual's primary social group on her political participation and choices.

Each chapter develops a different network measurement in an attempt to capture the general effects of political networks. In chapter 2, geography serves as a proxy for a social network. Individuals are likely to establish friendships based on geographic proximity. Individuals are more likely to know someone from their own five-digit zip code than another five-digit zip code. They are furthermore likely to know nearby neighbors in their nine-digit zip code. At the smallest level of geography, they most certainly know the people with whom they share a household address. Using geography as a proxy for social network ties has many benefits. First, it allows incorporation of both weak and strong ties. It does not require any particular individual to be able to recall his or her social network members or to respond to a particular survey, and thus it avoids potential problems of respondent recollection and survey nonresponse. Interestingly, however, the results presented in this chapter demonstrate that geography is a very weak proxy for a social network. While individuals do appear to be slightly affected by their household members, there is no evidence that they are affected by their neighbors.

The third chapter uses a behavioral measurement of the social network. Within a particular geography—a congressional district—individuals are considered to be connected if they donate to the same political organizations. This network definition relies weakly on shared geography (the congressional district) but advances the idea that a network is implicitly revealed by shared behavior. Individuals who donate to the same organizations may be acquainted by attending the same fundraisers or may never have met, but survey data conducted in this congressional district support the use of this implicit network measurement. As it turns out, however, this is a weak proxy. While it is true that individuals know codonors more frequently than noncodonors, they are only personally acquainted with one out of every twenty-five codonors on average.

The fourth and fifth chapters rely on a survey-based definition of networks. In these analyses, a national probability sample is drawn and surveyed: individuals are asked to identify a small number of other individuals who form their social network. The advantages of these survey responses are that they can incorporate network members from many different geographies and can locate the individuals whom the survey respondent believes are part of her social network. The disadvantages are that these include only strong ties and require the respondent to recall the names. While network definitions based on geography or behavior yield positive but weak effects of an individual's social networks on her political behavior, the survey results obtained using explicitly defined social networks generate stronger results.

Social Norms Via Social Pressure

This book demonstrates that ordinary citizens are influenced by their social networks both in their political choices and in their political participation decisions. The political networks in which each citizen is embedded—networks that develop for nonpolitical reasons—influence each citizen's decisions about whether to cast a ballot or identify with a party. This influence forces us to adjust our understanding of an individually based political calculus and generates a more complicated picture for democratic theory, as each individual reflects the combined preferences of her network and herself.

Participation in a democratic government can be represented by models in which individuals think collectively.[10] The interaction of social pressure and participatory democracy has three components: (1) Social networks affect our political behavior. (2) Particular kinds of network relationships, such as those with close social ties or where behavior is more publicly visible, have greater effects. (3) Social network effects are only present when the social network holds the behavior as part of a social norm. Of the three, the third component—that there must be a social norm in order for the behavior to spread—is the most important, because it is the principle that makes sense of the first two and that permits the greatest insight into why social networks affect political outcomes. Social norms are enforced through social pressure;

tracking the ways in which individuals can influence each other helps us to understand the extent to which an individual is a social citizen and confirms that the functioning of a democracy is attributable not merely to individual expression but to an expression of a collective social identity.

2   Voting Together: Do the Neighbors Know We Voted?

Across the country on Election Day, adults walk into polling places. When they emerge, many of them are wearing a sticker as a consequence of casting a ballot. The typical sticker, in bright patriotic colors, reads, "I VOTED!" The interesting question to investigate is why, after an election, so many voters wear these stickers. To whom do they want to demonstrate that they have a sticker, that they have voted? Whom do they want to notice these stickers and comment on their choice to participate in the election? Why is casting a ballot an act of public pride?

Voters wear the "I VOTED" stickers because they want to advertise to their social network that they have performed their civic duty. The "I VOTED" sticker demonstrates the social act of casting a ballot. Turning out to cast a ballot is a commonly held social norm, considered beneficial for the whole community.[1] Voters proudly display their stickers at the office, while running errands, while sitting at the dinner table. Across most avenues of life the voting sticker conjures up an image of a thoughtful, responsible citizen. It is not surprising that so many voters, then, would wistfully report they had cast a ballot when they in fact had not. Nationally, the high levels of overreporting of turnout by individuals in the ANES (about 20 percent) suggests that many people subscribe to a social norm of voting (Karp and Brockington 2005).

Yet although turning out to vote is socially desirable, not all voters have internalized a social norm of voting. That is, not everyone feels personally obligated to vote. Turnout in presidential elections throughout the 1990s, for example, is estimated at merely 50 percent of the registered voters (Karp and Brockington 2005). Yet many individuals appear to experience social pressure to vote. For example, the characteristics of those survey respondents who falsely report having cast a ballot are most similar to those of actual voters. This suggests that false reporters and actual voters are likely to experience similar environments as the actual voters and thus feel more social pressure to cast a ballot than those individuals who report having not voted (Silver, Anderson, and Abrahamson 1986). False reporting appears to stem in large part from social pressure to do so. For many citizens, failing to turn out to vote is a violation of the social network's political norms. Wearing the "I VOTED" sticker indicates compliance with the social norm of voting.

The Calculus of Social Voting

Why do citizens turn out to vote? The basic turnout model describes a calculus in which each individual decides whether or not to vote after considering the probability that her vote is pivotal, the relative benefit of her most preferred candidate winning, the costs of voting, and her sense of civic duty (Downs 1957; Riker and Ordeshook 1968). The classic scholarly literature on voting has demonstrated that varying these components affects turnout. For example, voters with higher socioeconomic status or more education, whose costs of turning out are lower, are more likely to cast a ballot (Verba and Nie 1972; Wolfinger and Rosenstone 1980). Similarly, when voters are part of larger electorates, and thus less likely to be pivotal, they are less likely to cast a ballot (Levine and Palfrey 2007). However, since the probability a voter is pivotal is typically quite small, while the costs of turning out are sizable, this turnout model generates the "paradox of voting." It is difficult to understand why so many individuals would cast a ballot if they expect that the costs will outweigh the benefits of turning out to vote.

The paradox of voting is resolved so long as voters rely upon social norms of civic duty to gain significant additional benefit from participating (Campbell, Gurin, and Miller 1954; Downs 1957; Riker and Ordeshook 1968; Gerber, Green, and Larimer 2008). There are two channels by which a voter's social environment can influence her calculus of voting. The first is the costs of participation. Voters can carpool to the polling place together, for example, and directly reduce each other's costs of voting. Voters can also share information about the candidates on the ballot or even about the election itself (the date of the election, the polling place location, etc.). This kind of information is likely to pass through social network ties as trusted information (Downs 1957) and is regularly transmitted through social networks such as civic groups (Rosenstone and Hansen 1993). Information provides one channel for social network influence.

The second channel, social pressure, is explored in this chapter. Voters are not intrinsically endowed with a sense of civic duty but rather establish a sense of their civic responsibilities from their social interactions. By varying the intensity with which they are reminded about civic responsibilities—whether by a family member who believes that voting is an imperative of any citizen or by a neighbor committed to increasing turnout for the community—it is possible to observe the extent to which an individual's utility is affected by shifts in civic duty. These shifts are attributable to increases in one's sense that voting is a social norm, and when these shifts are caused by interpersonal interactions, they are typically due to social pressure. The effects of these shifts is consistent with the scholarly literature on voter mobilization. Rosenstone and Hansen's (1993) claim attributing the decline in turnout to decreased mobilization campaigns, despite the lack of change in contact rates reported by survey respondents in the ANES (Abramson, Aldrich, and Rohde 1998), is consistent with this second channel having a larger effect than that of information. Campaigns' increased use of phone banks and direct-mail vendors provides information, not a sense of civic duty. Campaign contacts that simply provide information are not sufficient to substantially increase turnout, but more personalized contacts, which provide the social cue to maintain the social norm of voting, are more effective at getting out the vote (Gerber and Green 2000).

Most scholarly analysis on the calculus of voting considers the instrumental benefits and costs of voting but largely ignores the social element (Downs 1957; Riker and Ordeshook 1968; Brady, Verba, and Schlozman 1995; Timpone 1998). A few other scholars suggest an individual casts a ballot for other reasons. These include expressive motivations (Schuessler 2000), social influence (Rolfe 2012), and altruism (Fowler 2006a). There is some evidence of group pressure to cast a ballot as well. In an analysis of voter turnout in Japan, Cox, Rosenbluth, and Thies (1998) find that the probability of casting a ballot is affected by the social capital of the district. Fowler (2005b) describes a model that fits existing turnout data and is consistent with the data on explicit political discussion networks where there are voter-to-voter interactions in a network and each voter has a small probability of being affected by her social networks. Indirect mobilization is possible via group pressure to cast a ballot (Lipset 1960). Voting is likely to have a social component, where the desire of one individual to cast a ballot spills over to affect someone else in her social network.

Spillover effects are frequently discussed in the observational literature in political science. Many of these studies suggest the presence of a network effect but, largely as a result of data limitations, are unable to draw causal inferences that one network member affected the behavior of another. For example, the Erie County study (Berelson, Lazarsfeld, and McPhee 1954) reported that while just 8 percent of Elmira residents had been contacted, turnout increased by 10 percent, suggesting that mobilization contact was socially transmitted. Huckfeldt (1979) discusses the extent to which political activity occurs within a social context and the relationship between participation and social cues. His work suggests that people respond to political events, cues, and opportunities that are specific to a given social environment. Other scholars also have emphasized the influence of political discussion within individuals' social networks on their participation choices. Knoke (1990) finds that individuals with politicized social networks are more likely to engage politically. McClurg (2003) finds the information provided by those networks also to be key. Other researchers find a similar pattern (Bolton 1972; Briet, Klandermans, and Kroon 1987; Gerlach and Hine 1970; McAdam and Paulsen 1993; McAdam 1986). This work suggests that social networks influence an individual's subsequent decision to turn out and vote. Yet it is possible that these estimates suffer from the reflection problem (Manski 1993), wherein the outcomes of network neighbors may be correlated because they face common and unobserved shocks, rather than because they are communicating about politics.[2]

Social transmission of treatment effects have been observed in a handful of field experiments designed to look for spillover effects. Nickerson (2008) documents that 60 percent of the mobilization effect from door-to-door canvassing is carried over into the other household member in two-member households. Green, Gerber, and Nickerson (2003) find within-household spillover effects from door-to-door canvassing: an increase of 5.7 percentage points in the probability an individual voter turns out to vote for other household members among households of younger voters.[3] Yet it is not clear to which channel these effects are attributable: is each voter's information or sense of civic duty increased by spillover effect?

Recent field experiments have consistently noted the efficacy of publicly revealing whether or not a particular voter has adhered to the social norm of voting. These experiments, with stimuli ranging from mailing postcards listing a voter's publicly available history of electoral participation to threatening to publish nonvoter names in the local newspaper, have generated large mobilization effects comparable with the best door-to-door canvassing campaigns (Abrajano and Panagopoulos 2009; Gerber, Green, and Larimer 2008, 2010; Grose and Russell 2008; Larimer 2009; Mann 2010; Panagopoulos 2009, 2010; Sinclair, McConnell, and Green 2010). Dozens of other experiments have demonstrated that more personal mobilization stimuli (door-to-door conversations between a voter and a canvasser, for example, or a lengthy unscripted phone call) generate greater effects than more indirect methods, such as robocalls (Gerber and Green 2000, 2001; Green and Gerber 2008; Green, Gerber, and Nickerson 2003; Michelson, Bedolla, and McConnell 2009). The success of these experiments suggest that there are important social interactions at work behind the turnout decision. Voters fear they will lose some component of their social relationships—either status or respect—for failing to take part in the social norm of participating in democracy, that is, the civic duty of casting a ballot (Blais 2000).

Individuals are particularly likely to participate and comply with the social norm of voting when their decisions will be observed by their social network: neighbors, friends, or family who would notice the presence of the "I VOTED" stickers. Individuals are increasingly likely to participate in behaviors when their actions are observed (Harbaugh 1996; Cialdini and Trost 1998; Lerner and Tetlock 1999; Cialdini and Goldstein 2004). This effect is highlighted when members comply with social norms, and there are smaller to no effects when the attempt to cue social norms is from out-of-group references (Brehm and Brehm 1981). These patterns are seen, for example, in a field experiment providing encouragements regarding recycling—individuals who received information on recycling were much less likely to recycle than individuals who received information about the recycling behavior of their neighborhood (Schultz 1999).

Who Is Part of the Political Network?

It is difficult to assess social network membership across the many different ways in which people are connected to each other. Are the members of your social network the people with whom you spend your free time? Are they the people with whom you speak about important matters? Are they the people you talk to about politics? Do they live in your house, on your block, or in your neighborhood?

The experiments described in this chapter were designed to detect the effects of political networks, which are social networks in which individuals communicate about politics. The first place to look for political networks is within the immediate physical proximity of each individual. In the absence of evidence to the contrary, geographical proximity is likely to be a good proxy for places where political networks might exist. By locating people within the same household, the same nine-digit zip code, and the same five-digit zip code, it is possible to examine the extent to which geographically based networks determine an individual's political behavior. Using geography in conjunction with randomized experiments has some enormous advantages, in that it does not require any recall on the behalf of survey respondents but only that the network members engage in a shared political behavior that reveals the presence of the network connection.

In many counties, turning out to vote is a neighborhood activity. Polling places are located in each neighborhood in close proximity to the voters, and polling sites frequently include local homes, garages, churches, and schools. Social networks that affect turnout are more likely to be geographically based than those that affect other kinds of participation, since individual voters who are spatially proximate are likely to observe each other's participation. This is consistent with voting patterns in voter registration lists, where the neighborhood social context appears to have a direct effect on the probability of an individual's turnout (Cho, Gimpel, and Dyck 2006). Finally, network members who meet the individual in person are most likely to have an effect. In research on the influence of friends on Facebook, for example, Christakis and Fowler (2009) find that only those friends who have appeared in pictures together have influence over each other.

The sections that follow provide critical evidence that voting indeed has a social component and indicate that the mechanism driving social network effects is social pressure. The first section explains the operating definition of a social network. The next sections then describe two randomized field experiments that generate insight into the mechanism driving the social component of voting. In these experiments, voters respond to mobilization stimuli that is personal or that monitors their adherence to the social norm of voting. The behavior of these voters is compared to a similar set of voters who did not receive the mobilization stimuli. Since the stimulus was assigned at random to each voter, it is possible to compare the average turnout in the group that received the stimulus to the average turnout in the group that did not. In the two experiments presented in this chapter, comparisons between the two groups reveal positive effects on turnout that are attributable to social networks. Mobilization stimuli delivered by social network members generate higher levels of turnout than stimuli delivered by nonnetwork members, suggesting that social pressure drives compliance with the social norm of voting. Absent communication from individuals who have internalized the social norm of voting, there is little evidence of social spillover of the mobilization message between individuals in a social network. Yet evidence suggests that spillover between individuals occurs from an individual who wants compliance—who has internalized the norm—to someone else within the social network.

Using Experiments to Study Social Turnout

Randomized experiments are seen as the most rigorous methodology for testing causal explanations for phenomena in the social sciences. The classic experimental design randomly assigns the population of interest into two groups, treatment and control. Ex ante these two groups should have identical distributions in terms of their observed and unobserved characteristics. Treatment is administered based upon assignment, and, according to the assumptions of the Rubin Causal Model (Rubin 1974), the average effect of the treatment is calculated as the difference between the average outcome in the treatment group and the average outcome in the control group.

Voters are likely to communicate to others in their social network regarding their decision to cast a ballot. Spillover effects occur when the mobilization stimulus in an experiment is transmitted from one individual to another through such communications. To a large extent, the field experiment literature has ignored the possibility of this type of effect. This is in part because it is difficult to estimate such effects; the typical get-out-the-vote randomized field experiment estimates the effect of direct communication from the experimenters on turnout rather than the effect of communication about the mobilization treatment between individuals in the experiment. To observe a spillover effect it is necessary to design an experiment for that purpose.

Two possible design strategies allow estimation of the social effects. First, the experimenter can directly manipulate the social network. That is, the experimenter can treat some voters by ensuring that there are additional or new network ties who communicate a mobilization message and compare the voters who receive these new ties to those who do not. Second, the experimenter can stimulate some part of the network directly and then observe to what extent these manipulations spill over into other parts of the network. This chapter presents two experiments, each taking one of these approaches.

The next section describes an experiment that adopts the second design and allows for conversations within families and between neighbors to influence behavior. This design allows us to estimate the effect of potential communication about turnout between individuals via a multilevel experiment. In this experiment, there are three categories for the subjects—individuals who are socially isolated from the treatment, individuals who are socially proximate to the treatment, and individuals who receive the treatment. The subject population is randomly assigned to these three categories. By comparing turnout across the three groups it is possible to estimate the spillover effect, that is, the effect of the network indirectly delivering the treatment. This transforms what once was a methodological problem into a solution that both allows us to observe the extent to which individuals communicate about politics in the absence of selection concerns and estimates the effect of the direct treatment without biases introduced from such communication.

Study 1: Who Votes Is a Matter of Public Record
(Do Your Civic Duty and Vote!)

This experiment took place preceding the April 7, 2009, special election in the Fifth Congressional District of Illinois. This election was unusual in that there was only a single electoral contest on the ballot, for an open seat in the House of Representatives, with three candidates appearing on the ballot.[4] The contest received very little media coverage, and the candidates themselves did little campaigning, as the seat had historically been held by a Democrat and was not considered competitive.[5]

This electoral context provides an ideal venue to evaluate the effects of social norms on voter turnout. Most voters would have understood that their vote was unlikely to be instrumental in determining the election outcome for any particular candidate. That is, the utility of casting a ballot in this election without considering the social benefit from doing so was likely to be particularly low. As a consequence, if neighbors or families were to communicate about the election, they were unlikely to talk about the probability that any single vote would be pivotal in the outcome. Instead, political conversations were more likely centered on a normative desire to have higher turnout in an otherwise unsalient election. This electoral context provides a venue for individuals to focus their political conversations on the social norm of voting.

Experimental Population. The experimental population included a subset of all households in the Illinois Fifth Congressional District. Individuals were eligible to be part of the study if they had registered to vote before spring 2006 and lived in households where there were between one and three registered voters. The social structures of this type of households are likely very different from those of one-registered-voter households, which might consist of only one resident. A two-registered-voter household might consist of two spouses. A three-registered-voter household might consist of three roommates. Because of the possibility of these different social structures, the random assignment is stratified by household size, and results are presented based upon the number of registered voter residents.[6]

We relied upon individuals' 9-digit zip code as a proxy for their neighborhood. Nine-digit zip codes consist of a five-digit zip code plus a four-digit number that identifies a compact geographic segment within the five-digit delivery area, such as a city block, office building, or individual high-volume receiver of mail (Maponics 2010). Our use of nine-digit zip codes was intended to capture very local neighborhoods. Each nine-digit zip code in our study comprised roughly fifteen eligible voters. Some nine-digit zip codes included a single apartment building, and the largest comprised one city block 0.2 miles long. The purpose of nine-digit zip codes, initiated in 1983, is to aid efficient mail sorting and delivery (Grubesic 2008; Grubesic and Matisziw 2006). The average distance between the residences of any two study participants within the same nine-digit zip code is sixty feet. For our study 71,127 individuals, 47,851 households, and 4,897 zip codes were eligible.

Randomization and the Multilevel Design. In order to assess the influence of different audiences who will exert social pressure, the experimental design incorporated randomization at multiple levels. The multilevel random assignment corresponded to places where there are likely to be social interactions that could result in indirect treatment via spillover. This allows evaluation of the relative impact, for example, of the larger community in contrast to the household. Randomization at multiple levels allows us to examine places where we believed treatment spillover was likely—that is, where the treatment was likely to be socially communicated within a political network. Like the classic experimental design, the multilevel experimental design randomly assigns the population of interest into multiple groups: those who directly receive treatment, those who may indirectly receive treatment, and control (Sinclair 2010; Sinclair, McConnell, and Green 2010). The advantage of randomization to multiple groups is that an additional inference can also be drawn, which is the spillover effect. This is calculated as the difference between the average outcome in the group assigned to indirectly receive treatment and the average outcome in the group assigned to control. This design can be extended to many different types of indirect treatment groups. This experiment focuses on indirect treatment of household members and neighbors within a nine-digit zip code.

In this experiment, randomization occurred in both the nine-digit zip code area and in the household. Imagine two identical households, each with two registered voters. In one household, one of the voters received the treatment (a postcard). The comparison we are interested in drawing is not between the individual who received the postcard and those who did not but between the individual in the household where one resident was treated who did not receive the postcard and the individuals in the other household. By comparing the individual who was eligible to be indirectly treated to an individual who was not, it is possible to observe whether there is a spillover effect from receiving the postcard. We conducted this experiment not only across household members for one-, two-, and three-person households, but also across neighborhoods. Some nine-digit zip codes contained households where no residents received a postcard, and only one household received a postcard in some others (classified as the "low" neighborhood treatment); in some, half of the households receive a postcard (classified as the "medium" neighborhood treatment), and in some all but one of the households receive a postcard (classified as the "high" neighborhood treatment). The treatment intensity of the neighborhood as well as the particular voters who received postcards were randomly assigned.[7] This random assignment eliminates concerns over selection effects—that individuals will appear to behave similarly not because one influences the other but because they have become social network ties because of their similarities. This makes it possible to identify the extent to which there is a causal effect by perturbing the behavior of one network member who was randomly selected and then observing the behavior of the other network members in the household and in the neighborhood.

Postcard Treatment. In the final week before the April 2009 special election, approximately twenty thousand registered voters in the Illinois

```
Dear Richard L Jensen:

DO YOUR CIVIC DUTY AND VOTE ON APRIL 7!

Why do so many people fail to vote?  We've been talking about
this problem for years, but it only seems to get worse --
especially when elections are held in the spring.

This year we're taking a different approach.  We're reminding
people that who votes is a matter of public record.  The chart
shows your name from the list of registered voters and whether
you voted in the last two spring elections.  The chart also
contains an empty space that we will fill in based on whether
you vote in the April 7th election.

DO YOUR CIVIC DUTY AND VOTE ON APRIL 7!

VOTER NAME                    Spring 2006  Spring 2008   April 7
RICHARD L JENSEN              Didn't Vote  Didn't Vote  _____
```

FIGURE 2.1. Sample postcard

Fifth Congressional District received a postcard in the mail reminding them to do their civic duty and participate in spring elections.[8] Similar to the experimental postcard sent by Gerber, Green, and Larimer (2008), the postcard in this study explicitly named a recipient and indicates his or her voting history for the previous spring 2006 and spring 2008 elections, leaving a line for the April 2009 election blank. Postcards were mailed only to those residents who had been eligible to participate in both the 2006 and 2008 spring elections (see figure 2.1). Each postcard reveals to the voter that her turnout behavior is a matter of public record and holds her accountable to the social norm of voting.

This type of postcard mailer has generated high increases in voter turnout in previous elections. Gerber, Green, and Larimer (2008) used a similar postcard in a Michigan election and increased turnout by 8.1 percent. Why do these postcards generate such high turnout? One possibility is that when a voter's history of participation is publicly revealed, the voter feels social pressure to participate. This pressure could be exerted by household members who might also see the postcard or even by neighbors who are more likely to communicate about prior voting history after receiving the postcard. Who exerts the social pressure is of interest in this experiment, where those who may exert social pressure include household members and nearby neighbors.

Spillover Effects. The experimental design of this study allows measurement of spillover within individuals' social networks by incorporating a multilevel randomization. This strategy allows us to estimate both direct and indirect effects of the stimulus. We estimated the magnitude of spillovers within households and across households within zip codes but found little evidence of spillovers.

We analyzed results by household size and estimated the direct effect of receiving the postcard treatment, the indirect effect of having some-one else in the household receive the treatment, and the indirect effect of having neighbors treated with the various levels of nine-digit zip code treatments (low, medium, and high). Each of these coefficients is plotted in figure 2.2, where the black dots indicate the coefficients estimated in the regression analysis and the horizontal lines indicate the 95 percent confidence intervals. The coefficient represents the increased probability that individuals will cast a ballot if they are exposed to the stimulus, either directly or indirectly, that is described by the label on the left. An individual who lives in a household with one other registered voter who received the postcard is exposed to a household effect in a two-person household, labeled Household Effect (2 PH), for example, has an increased likelihood of turnout, but the 95 percent confidence interval includes zero, so the effect is not statistically significant.

Each of these estimates can be interpreted as an intent-to-treat effect (ITT), that is, the average difference between the category described on the y-axis and a pristine control group. It was not possible to know which individuals actually received or read it, nor is it possible to know which individuals communicated about the postcard with other residents of their household or zip code. There are likely many individuals, for example, whose spouse read the postcard. In these instances—because of the possibility that someone else in the household could be indirectly treated by reading the postcard—the estimates for spillover have the potential to be positive beyond the potential effects of communication.

As seen in figure 2.2, the intended recipients of the postcard were more likely to turn out to cast a ballot. Turnout increased between 3 and 5 percent depending on the size of the household; this effect is sta-tistically significant and robust to the inclusion of covariates.[9]

However, we see very little evidence for any type of spillover effect. In figure 2.2, the neighborhood effects are broken out by household size and the intensity with which the neighborhood was treated. Regardless of household size or the intensity of the nine-digit zip code treatment, it is not possible to distinguish the neighborhood spillover effects from zero: the 95 percent confidence intervals of all possible neighborhood spillovers include zero. Thus it does not appear that individuals com-municated with their neighbors about voting. Given the potential of a household member reading the mail or the ability to share the costs of

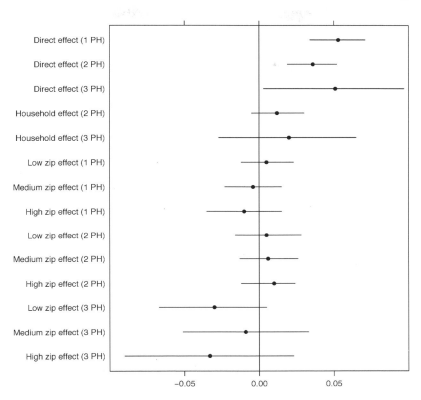

FIGURE 2.2. Regression estimates of treatment and spillover effects by household size
   Numbers preceding "PH" indicate the number of registered voters in respondents' households. Dots indicate point estimates, and bars indicate the 95 percent confidence intervals.

voting in some way (either by carpooling or sharing information about the upcoming election), we expected to observe evidence of a household effect. In figure 2.2 these effects are broken out by household size, but while their magnitude suggests a household spillover effect, as the point estimates for both two- and three-person households are positive, the 95 percent confidence intervals include zero.

   Yet social voting is likely to be moderated in two key ways. First, voting is habitual (Gerber, Green, and Shachar 2003; Green and Shachar 2000; Miller and Shanks 1996; Plutzer 2002; Verba and Nie 1972). Individuals who exert social pressure need to have a history of voting; we focused on those individuals who live in households with others who have already succumbed to the social norm of turning out. Second, because voting is habitual, we expected to observe effects among those who don't typically vote. That is, we anticipated effects in a more limited context: we expected the effect to spill over from voters who habitually turn out to voters who seldom cast a ballot.

Theoretically, the mechanism driving this expected result is social pressure. In this case individuals who have not internalized the social norm of voting will not communicate about the postcard without an explicit social cue. While individuals will respond to the direct mobilization stimulus, given that their behavior is being observed, they will not encourage others to turn out to vote. Only particular types of individuals are likely to be exposed to social pressure: those with one or more housemates who had internalized the social norm of voting. Individuals who lived with registered voters who had participated in many previous elections would experience larger direct treatment effects than individuals who lived with registered voters who had not participated in many previous elections. The treatment effects would be particularly large if the postcard revealed that the housemate had not participated in previous spring elections. Individuals who received the postcards would be exposed as having not voted, and those who lived with someone who had internalized the social norm of voting would experience greater effects.[10]

According to this argument, it is necessary to examine differential effects resulting from the message in the postcard. Analysis of the direct treatment effect is then stratified based upon whether the subject had failed to participate in one or both of the elections listed on the postcard and whether the housemate had participated in at least four of the previous elections. The coefficients from this analysis are presented in figure 2.3. Among those whose postcards indicated participation in one or neither of the previous elections, those who lived with housemates who had participated in four previous elections were likely to experience a greater direct treatment effect.

These coefficients are not statistically distinguishable from each other, but they do provide suggestive evidence for the social pressure mechanism, based upon expression of a social norm. This is weak evidence of social pressure—individuals are more likely to participate if they live with someone who has a history of participating, particularly if they themselves have low voter turnout reported on the postcard. This suggests that the audience, person, or group who administers the social pressure must have internalized the social norm of voting and is likely to have close network ties with those upon whom pressure is exerted. More direct evidence is needed to assess to what extent a single individual motivates her social networks to participate. The next experiment varies the messenger who administers the treatment and ensures that

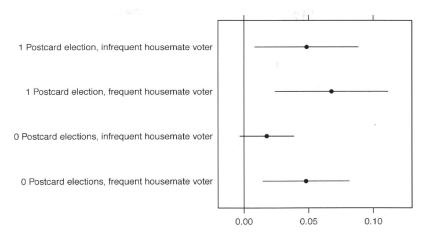

FIGURE 2.3. Regression estimates of individual treatment by housemate vote history and postcard participation

Dots indicate point estimates, and bars indicate the 95 percent confidence intervals. Individuals could have their participation in up to two previous elections printed on their postcard. A frequent housemate voter is defined as one who participated in more than four of the nine previous elections. All estimates are based upon one individual and two-person household.

this person is committed to the social norm of voting. This strengthens the argument for social pressure.

Study 2: The Neighbors Are at the Door (Mobilization by Local Canvassing)

Suppose voters are motivated by social pressure. Suppose many voters cast ballots not because they themselves adhere to a social norm of voting but because they are aware that some people do hold such beliefs, and they do not want to lose the benefits of those social connections. Then individual voters should be more likely to participate if the mobilization stimulus is delivered by someone they know who genuinely believes that voting is a necessary component of one's civic duty—that is, someone who has internalized the social norm of voting. This experiment is designed to test social pressure by varying the type of canvasser who went door-to-door to mobilize voters.

Individuals from a pool of low-propensity voters in South Los Angeles were randomly assigned either to be contacted by a canvasser or to receive no contact. Two different categories of canvassers were used in the experiment: local canvassers and nonlocal canvassers. Because the experiment held the mobilization message constant but varied the social proximity of the canvasser to the voter, it is possible to ascertain to what degree social proximity affects turnout.[11]

Local and nonlocal canvassers were similar; all were volunteers helping a grassroots political organization called Strategic Concepts in Organizing and Political Education (SCOPE) increase voter turnout in South Los Angeles. Both types of canvassers lived in South Los Angeles, so they were equally familiar with the general area. Both types of canvassers wore identical yellow T-shirts with their organization's label on the back and a name tag on the front. Both types of canvassers read an identical script designed to mobilize voters. The sole difference between local canvassers and nonlocal canvassers was their home zip code.

While neighborhoods are often nebulous entities and hard to define geographically, zip codes are an appropriate proxy for neighborhoods for several reasons, particularly in South Los Angeles. The postal service designates zip codes based upon geographically compact areas for mail delivery. Unlike precinct boundaries, zip codes do not change with election cycles and may more closely resemble the geographic boundaries of a neighborhood. Zip codes are a common proxy for neighborhoods in a variety of fields of study, including medicine, economics, and political science (e.g., Boslaugh et al. 2004; Aizer and Currie 2004; Gould 1986; Powell et al. 2007; Ku, Sonenstein, and Pleck 1993). In South Los Angeles, zip codes are especially appropriate, given the nature of the larger community. Many residents of the area do not have personal automobiles, and a significant amount of activity within the neighborhood is thus confined to walkable distances. The average zip code in the area is 3.9 square miles in size and contains an average of 1,580 occasional voters (Garcia and Pitkin 2007). In other words, residents of this community are likely to do their grocery shopping within their zip code (walking to a local convenience store rather than driving to a larger supermarket) and to socialize within their zip code at parks and with their immediate neighbors. Individuals sharing a zip code might not know each other personally but likely would recognize many of their local canvassers from the local store or park. This is confirmed by anecdotal accounts from SCOPE canvassers, who reported that they personally knew many of their targets when canvassing their own zip codes.

The script used by canvassers during the campaign was designed to cue compliance with the social norm of voting by referencing an individual's social neighborhood network. Canvassers spoke of the importance of issues on the ballot to "our community." Regardless of whether canvassers were working their own zip code, they told contacted voters: "We're out today talking to our neighbors about the upcoming elections" and then went on to say, "This is an important election. There are lots of issues on the ballot that impact our neighborhoods. We want to make sure our community demonstrates our power by turning out to vote." The script concluded, "SCOPE is a grassroots organization building power in our neighborhoods. We believe that the only way we'll be able to change the conditions in our community is by getting organized and taking action."

Because all canvassers used the same script, it is possible to isolate the effect of using locals versus nonlocals as canvassers. That is, this is a clear test of the two mechanisms of information and social pressure. On one hand, the canvassers provide information. All contacted voters received the same information and were given similar cues as to the importance of the election and the social norm of participating. However, those contacted by local canvassers were more likely to know or recognize the canvasser as someone from their own neighborhood. As Rosenstone and Hansen (1993:23) observe, "People in these networks reward those who comply with expectations, and they sanction those who do not. . . . For most people, the obligations and rewards of friendship, camaraderie, neighborliness, and family ties are very powerful. People want to be accepted, valued, and liked." Local canvassing increases the likelihood the canvasser and voter will interact again in the future and that a lack of conformity to the social norm of voting may be observed by the local canvasser. That all individuals receive the same information but the type person delivering the information will vary will illustrate the effect of a social network on turnout. It will also help clarify the mechanism by which social networks affect political behavior. Gerber, Green, and Larimer (2008) look at the role of social norms, but they do not include the impact of an individual's social network. That is, while norms are invoked, there is no audience. This experiment allows for the first causal explanation of why individuals are motivated by references to such norms, and the results are highly consistent with a social pressure mechanism.

Local Effects. To assess the effect of the experiment, we estimated the ITT and the treatment-on-treated effect (TOT), using validated voter turnout data obtained from the Los Angeles County registrar. The ITT is the observed difference in turnout between those assigned to the treatment and control groups. The TOT is equivalent to the ITT divided by the contact rate (see Green and Gerber 2008). Turnout among those assigned to the treatment group was 36.7 percent, compared to 33.7 percent in the control group, for an ITT of 3.0 percent. Using two-stage least squares, we estimate a TOT of 6.6 percent. That is, individuals

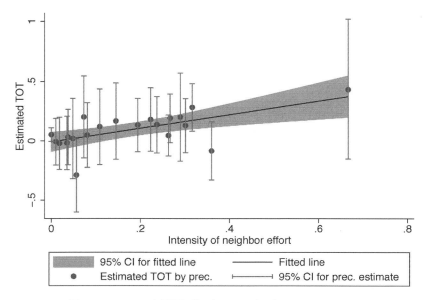

FIGURE 2.4. Treatment-on-treated (TOT) effect by percent local canvassing
Each dot represents one precinct. Only those precincts with more than zero local canvassing are represented in this figure.

who received a canvasser were 6.6 percent more likely to turn out to cast a ballot.

We then examined the relationship between precinct-level TOT estimates and the intensity of local canvassing (see figure 2.4). Dots demonstrate the precinct-level estimates of the local treatment, with the bars representing the 95 percent confidence interval for each precinct estimate. The x-axis demonstrates the intensity of the local effort—the fraction of individuals in that precinct who were contacted by a local canvasser. The solid line (the measurement of the amount of turnout given that fraction of local canvassing) is fit through the precinct estimates (the dots), with the gray shading demonstrating the 95 percent confidence interval for the fitted line. In this figure, the line has a clearly positive slope: as the intensity of the local effort increases, turnout increases.[12] The greater the fraction of individuals who were successfully contacted by a local canvasser, the higher the turnout. Analysis of only those individuals who were successfully contacted is included in table 2.1.

This campaign was successful partly because it was directed by a grassroots organization that is well established in the community and has a well-developed get-out-the-vote infrastructure. It is able to recruit volunteers who are part of the community's social network and can conduct a high-quality, personal campaign. People are able to mobilize other people. While Gerber and Green (2000) find that door-to-door campaigning is more effective than phone calls, this experiment provides direct evidence as to why. Individuals are more willing to bear the cost of voting to maintain their social connections than they are as a result of simply being given information. In this experiment, the team of door-to-door canvassers increased turnout in targeted neighborhoods of South Los Angeles for the November 2006 election by approximately a 6.6 percent. More important, there is a significant increase in turnout as a result of local canvassing. Local canvassers mobilize more effectively than nonlocal canvassers.

Turnout is not completely driven by social network effects. Yet the effectiveness of local canvassers tells us that social networks in local

Table 2.1. OLS Coefficients: Effect of Local Contact on Turnout by Contacted Individuals

Variable	OLS	OLS with control variables	OLS with canvasser-specific effects	OLS with canvasser-specific effects and control variables
Local contact	0.056*	0.044**	0.113**	0.094*
	(0.024)	(0.025)	(0.031)	(0.031)
Democratic registration		0.009		0.011
		(0.015)		(0.015)
Age		0.001*		0.001
		(0.000)		(0.000)
Missing age		−0.025		−0.022
		(0.036)		(0.036)
Female		−0.015		−0.014
		(0.018)		(0.018)
Missing female		0.079		0.065
		(0.147)		(0.148)
Vote history		0.175**		0.174**
		(0.007)		(0.007)
Latino		0.127**		0.122**
		(0.023)		(0.023)
Precinct fixed effects		Included		Included
Walker fixed effects			Included	Included
Constant	0.307**	0.108**	0.500**	0.215
	(0.050)	(0.023)	(0.174)	(0.163)
F (covariates)	5.23	17.16	3.05	10.28
N	5,343	5,343	5,343	5,343

Note: There is a separate fixed effect coefficient for contacts made by unknown walkers (399 observations). "Local contact" indicates contact from a canvasser who was a resident of the same ZIP code as the voter. The dependent variable is whether or not the contacted individual turned out to vote. Standard errors are shown in parentheses.
* $\alpha = .05$.
** $\alpha = .10$.

communities play key roles in driving political participation. Social networks are linked to political behavior. Neighbors are more effective than individuals from other neighborhoods, even within a larger community.

Evidence of Social Pressure

The results from the two experiments in this chapter uncover social network effects as a likely causal mechanism in political behavior. The empirical findings from both experiments are consistent with a pattern of social pressure. In the first experiment, there is little support for spillover effects. Neighbors are unlikely to vote together. Household residents are only weakly affected by each other's choices. However, the mere efficacy of the postcard, which increased individual-level turnout by 3 to 5 percent for those who received the postcard directly, suggests that individuals want to conform to social norms, particularly once they realize those behaviors are publicly visible. There are also suggestive patterns with respect to individuals who are differentially affected by the postcard with respect to their housemate voting patterns. Treated individuals who receive a postcard that reveals that they have failed to participate in the previous spring elections but who live with housemates who have a history of voting are more likely to participate than those who live with housemates who typically do not vote. The differential effects—based upon the norm held by the housemate—suggest that the treated individuals base some component of their turnout decision on the preferences of their social connections. Individuals are more likely to vote if their housemates know their voting patterns.

The social-pressure effect is illustrated in the experiment that varied the type of canvasser. Here, canvassers were sometimes neighbors—members of the immediate community. They read a script designed to inform the voter about the social norm of participation to which the community adhered. Neighbors are more effective at delivering this message than strangers. That social conformity can be instigated by a member of the local community suggests that neighbors are more effective because of social pressure. Simply delivering this notification without being a network member has a smaller effect.

Because individuals choose their housemates and their neighbors, it is important to recall that this chapter illustrates one of the benefits of randomization. In the multilevel experiment, it is possible to compare the turnout behavior of individuals who are indirectly treated by their housemates and neighbors to individuals who are not indirectly treated.

The level of correlation in voting patterns between housemates and between neighbors is extremely high, so one advantage of the random assignment of treatment is that it resolves one of the many problems that homophily poses in establishing evidence for social network effects. In both experiments, the advantages of the designs are that there are exogenous manipulations of the network. The disadvantages of these experiments are that social networks are measured based upon geographic proximity. One explanation for the weak neighborhood results is that individuals are only influenced by those with whom they talk about politics, and these individuals may not be neighbors. The subsequent chapters in this book attempt to establish network ties using alternative strategies, ranging from shared behavior to self-identified networks. Across chapters, there is evidence that close ties are more likely to produce network effects. The weak household effects are consistent with this theory. Interestingly, the findings presented in this chapter suggest that those who subscribe to the social norm of voting are most likely to be effective at increasing turnout in others.

One individual can motivate others to turn out to vote. As stated by Rosenstone and Hansen (1993: 27, 29–30), "The impact of political mobilization . . . extends far beyond the effect it has on the limited number of people who are contacted directly. . . . Thus, by working through social networks political leaders need not provide selective incentives themselves, need not coax, cajole, and persuade people to take part. Social networks do it for them. Family, friends, neighbors, and coworkers echo leaders' calls to action, and participants respond to please their neighbors and coworkers and to honor their obligations to friends. Working through social networks, politicians, parties, interest groups, and activists piggyback political action onto the everyday hum of social relationships." Social networks can effectively spread the social norm of voting.

What other social norms are contagious within social networks? This chapter documents that individuals overcome the costs of voting and cast a ballot based upon their obligations to friends. Friendship is also associated with a willingness to bear other types of costs, particularly willingness to donate money to a political campaign. Who should be willing to bear these costs? Experimental turnout results suggest it is those who have personal relationships with donors who have internalized the social norm of contributing to campaigns.

3

Social Campaign Giving: Could You Please Take Out Your Checkbook?

Why was the Obama campaign so successful at online fundraising? The My.BarackObama.com website set up by the Obama campaign leveraged supporters' social connections to establish a fundraising base comprising networks of personal friends. Unlike traditional campaign websites where candidates post information for supporters to read, the My.BarackObama.com website allowed individuals to communicate with each other to form an online community of supporters. The website encouraged users to "find local events and groups, contact undecided voters near you and share your story on your blog." Members of the website described themselves and their reasons for wanting to support Obama in a "profile" and used the site to connect to other Obama supporters. This website was terrifically effective at encouraging participation and donation. At the close of the campaign in November 2008, MyBarackObama.com had over a million and a half members (Bellini 2008). In February 2008 alone, the Obama campaign raised $55 million, $45 million of it online (J. Green 2008).

This site encouraged people to bring their personal relationships online. Within each individual's preexisting social network, the website allowed the formation of a political network. The campaign used that network to produce additional fundraising by encouraging individuals to contact their friends and ask them to donate to the campaign. According to Obama staffer and Facebook cofounder Chris Hughes, "The scale and size of this community and its work is unprecedented. Individuals in all 50 states have created more than 35,000 local organizing groups, hosted over 200,000 events and made millions upon millions of calls to neighbors about this campaign. There can be no question that these local, grassroots organizations played a critical role in Tuesday's victory" (Havenstein 2008).

The groups formed by these online political networks were designed to move people from online participation to real-world participation. For example, one of the website's tools allowed individuals to download a list of their neighbors whom the Obama campaign had identified as potential supporters. The website encouraged users to go to those individuals and speak for a few moments about Obama and the campaign. It then provided the users with a form to relay the results of those conversations back to the campaign—turning each user into a very small grassroots campaign operation. By confirming each participant's value to the campaign, the website positively affected the participation of each user. More crucial to the success of the website, however, was that this campaign allowed individuals to establish norms of political participation within their preexisting social networks. The focus of this participation was campaign giving.

The success of My.BarackObama.com is attributable to two components. First, the website encouraged social interactions among users' preexisting social relationships. Many of these social relationships are the result of nonpolitical interactions, and thus the campaign did not have to develop relationships between users. Second, the website made campaign donation a public act. Donating to the campaign was then observed within these social relationships, and social group members expected each other to contribute. That is, campaign donations became a social norm within these groups: a rule of behavior that imposed uniformity within the social group: given the expectation of conformity, most people preferred to conform (Durlauf and Blume 2010, s.v. "Social Norms"). The campaign website neither dictated the social norm of giving nor generated social ties between individuals. It simply provided a forum where preexisting social relationships could become political relationships and publicized the giving patterns of users. Donations increased as a consequence.

The growth of social networking websites in political campaigns underscores the need to understand the structure of who communicates with whom during the course of a campaign and how individuals are persuaded to donate to campaigns. Do friends notice campaign donations? When are donations explicitly social? Other campaign organizations have also developed to take advantage of social ties, such as the Democratic National Committee's website PartyBuilder.com and the Republican National Committee's website GOP.com, both of which allow users to post a profile, contribute, and make online social connections. Toward the end of the 2008 presidential campaign, the social networking website Facebook allowed individuals to post their "status" to remind people to turn out to vote or to express support for particular candidates, and more than 1.7 million users posted a "status" in favor of a particular candidate (Bellini 2008). This arena of political campaigning is rapidly changing because of new technologies available to voters and supporters, but these new technologies take advantage of the social component of political behavior, which existed before the development of online social networking websites. This chapter explores the social component of campaign contributions.

When Is Campaign Giving Social Giving?

Why do people donate to political campaigns? Are campaign donations rational investments in political outcomes? Some scholars suggest that campaign gifts affect policy outcomes, in which case donors might contribute to campaigns for a purely instrumental reason: if donors choose to invest in a candidate, then the candidate may shift policy consistent with the donation patterns (Snyder 1990) or actually change his or her roll-call vote (Silberman and Durden 1976; Kau, Keenan, and Rubin 1982; Chappell 1982). Donor choices suggest that they believe they affect policy outcomes: donors make out-of-district contributions more frequently where they have an increased possibility of exerting influence over party control of seats, indicating that their donations may be highly strategic (Gimpel, Lee, and Pearson-Merkowitz 2008; Bednar and Gerber 2011). In their extensive study of participation, Rosenstone and Hansen (1993) maintain that donors contribute based upon individual strategic political motivations (such as the similarity between their personal ideology and the political candidate). If the donor receives a direct benefit from contributing or has a reasonable belief that the contribution is pivotal, she may rationally choose to invest in a campaign. However, other scholars have refuted arguments that a particular individual's gift is pivotal or that individuals are likely to receive a direct political benefit from their contribution. Approximately 10 percent of

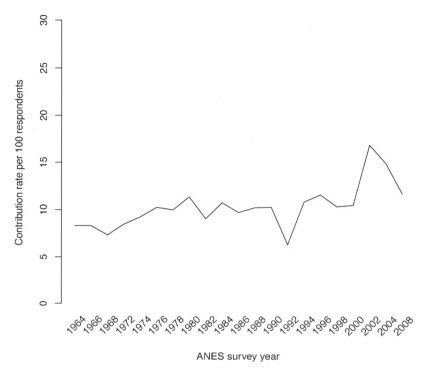

FIGURE 3.1. Political contributions over time

This rate reflects whether the survey respondent on the ANES indicated she had made any political contribution, although it explicitly does not include public financing of political campaigns via federal income tax returns.

the respondents to the ANES typically donate to some kind of political campaign or organization (Ho et al. 2007a, 2007b). These results can be seen in figure 3.1.

   With so many individuals likely to donate, why would any particular individual feel compelled to do so? If donors are motivated to give based upon the possibility of changing a policy outcome, then campaigns are subject to a classic problem of collective action, where it is not possible to prevent nondonors from also benefitting from the donor's contribution. However, in survey responses, donors do not appear to believe another individual's gift or federal campaign funding could substitute for their gift (Bergstrom, Blume, and Varian 1986; Andreoni 1988). Furthermore, there is little evidence that a donor could plausibly believe his or her gift is pivotal, as only very large amounts of money could affect election outcomes. For example, it would take an increase of approximately $100,000 to change the victory margin by 1 percent in a typical House race (Jacobson 1980; Levitt 1994).

Individuals are also unlikely to receive a political benefit from their contribution. There is very little clear empirical evidence suggesting that campaign gifts affect policies or votes of candidates. As Ansolabehere, deFigueiredo, and Snyder (2003, 12) observe, "It seems highly unlikely that 21 million individual donors giving an average of $115 apiece were calculating the return that they would personally receive on this investment." Do campaign donations present another paradox of participation, like voting, where neither the probability of making the pivotal gift nor the explicit political benefit is sufficiently high to explain the preponderance of campaign donations?

There is an additional reason that individuals donate to campaigns that relates to the success of the Obama webpage. Sometimes individuals donate to campaigns because their friends donate. People often donate to an organization not because they are looking for an opportunity to strategically invest in a policy outcome but simply because a friend asks them to donate. Whether this involves sponsoring a friend in a 10K race or buying cookies from a neighbor's Girl Scout troop, some donations are a consequence of personal influence. Campaigns specifically encourage their supporters to leverage their social connections to recruit additional donors, and personal requests appear to be particularly effective at generating donations (Brady, Schlozman, and Verba 1999; Grant and Rudolph 2002). This is the social component of campaign giving.

There are two key theories regarding socially motivated gifts. The first is that individuals donate to adhere to social norms, whether descriptive (what most people do) or injunctive (what people ought to do). Individuals typically want to conform to social norms—some they have internalized, while others they have not, but regardless they still want to align themselves with the appropriate social behaviors of their social network (Gerber, Green, and Larimer 2008). Experimentally, providing individuals with information about the donation behavior of their social networks does generate conformity, suggesting that social comparisons with respect to donation choices motivate giving (Shang and Croson 2006; Karlan and McConnell 2009). Frey and Meier (2004) conducted a randomized field experiment surrounding a mail fundraising campaign run by a university, where some students receive a letter telling them that 64 percent of other students had previously contributed (representing the number who actually contributed in the last year), while other students receive a letter telling them that 46 percent of other students had previously contributed (representing the number who actually contributed over the last ten years). Seventy-seven percent of students in the 64 percent treatment contribute to the fund, while 74.7 percent of students in the 46 percent treatment contribute. Similar results are generated with experiments surrounding patterns of donation to National Public Radio (Shang and Croson 2010; Shang, Croson, and Reed 2010) and participation in environmental efforts, such as recycling and energy consumption (Schultz 1999; Schultz et al. 2007; Bolsen 2010). Additionally, as the gift becomes more publicly visible, individuals are motivated to donate more (Andreoni and Bernheim 2009; Bénabou and Tirole 2006; Andreoni 1989; Linardi and McConnell 2009). This pattern is similar to individuals' decisions about voting and recycling when given additional social information (Feddersen and Sandroni 2009; Feddersen, Gailmard, and Sandroni 2009). Social norms can exert influence through social learning by observation without explicit direct communication from one network member to another.

The second theory is that individuals donate because of social interaction with individuals within their social network. Fundraising professionals claim that people do not give to causes but to other people (Tempel 2003). Individuals sustain their network relationships by maintaining the same participatory behaviors as those within their social network; in the case of campaign giving, this implies donating to the same types of organizations with the same frequency and magnitude as their network peers, even as their networks alter (Croson and Shang 2011). These donations are key signals to the network that the individual subscribes to the social norms valued by the network. Social networks play a key role in a variety of political participation behaviors, as maintaining network social norms, including those that involve a citizen's political obligations, is a key component of social network membership.

Whether the primary origin of the social influence is internal or external norms, however, the important distinction is that these are explicitly social influences as opposed to the influence of information. Individuals adhere to a set of behaviors in order to behave like the individuals in their social networks. Social networks characterize a range of different political behaviors, from candidate choice to the decision to turn out to vote. The primary mechanism that drives these effects is social influence, as behaviors that are stimulated by personal contact directly link individual behavior with that of a group or originate from close social ties (Gerber and Green 2000; Gerber, Green, and Larimer 2008). Social influence specifically appears to encourage behaviors that are consistent with social norms (Cialdini and Goldstein 2004; Cialdini and Trost

1998; Scheff 2000). A corollary to this theory, then, is that campaign giving should be contagious across social relationships, even though it does not appear to achieve an instrumental purpose.

There are other theories regarding socially motivated gifts. Donations that are publicly visible, for example, may be an attempt by the donor to signal to social networks her wealth and status (Harbaugh 1998; Glazer and Konrad 1996; Veblen 1899). When individual gifts are observed by their social networks, individuals may also donate as a way to strategically signal to social networks the importance of the particular cause (Vesterlund 2003). Yet these explanations for socially motivated giving are difficult to reconcile with the empirical support for the influence of social norms and social networks. Individuals likely make donations for many reasons, and the focus of this chapter is the extent to which their innate sociability stimulates campaign donations.

Social Network Effects and Political Contributions

Social networks are key for a range of political behaviors, and network effects are very likely to stimulate campaign giving. However, existing research is typically unable to distinguish between specific targeting by campaigns or shared characteristics of the donors and true social network effects. This chapter presents evidence of social network effects in campaign giving. By comparing individuals' political campaign donations with individual-level demographic variables and zip code–level socioeconomic and demographic variables, it is possible to understand the ways in which individual-giving patterns correspond to the political network. Additional control variables help to parse out the effects of shared characteristics and allow the chapter to focus on shared patterns of giving among individuals. Giving patterns observed by incorporating additional public records and personal interviews with donors suggest the presence of social network effects. Two sets of evidence support this claim.

First, there is weak evidence of social network effects in political contributions when all publicly recorded donations in a single congressional district are aggregated and the rate of cogiving between individuals as a proxy for a social network connection between donors is isolated. All publicly recorded campaign donations from residents of the district discussed in this chapter and its environs to federal candidates and political action committees from June 2006 to January 2009 are aggregated into a single data set, and census data along with individual-level voting history data are merged into this file. A donation network is then observed, where two individuals are linked by their donation to a common campaign or organization. The pattern of donations among individuals provides evidence of giving patterns that are consistent with the presence of social network effects in campaign giving. These descriptive statistics generate insights into who contributes to which organizations and what types of gifts are typical. These summaries are based entirely on a group of individuals who have already made the decision to contribute. The statistical analysis then focuses on whether or not social networks influence additional giving, not whether social networks generate any donations whatsoever.

Second, interview data conducted with individual donors suggest that, along with information that is transmitted between social network members about opportunities to give, social influence elicits donations from these individuals as well. Individuals report that cogiving maintains social status and reputation and sustains a social donor network. The presence of social network effects in campaign giving is indicative of the role that social networks play in establishing norms of behavior. Survey data from the donors in this congressional district confirm that social relationships between codonors exist and that many of the donors belong to family and friendship networks in which there is a norm of campaign giving. Donors who know each other make donations more closely timed together. These are critical tests for the social influence mechanism.

The method of indirectly identifying a political network from contribution data is discussed in the sections that follow. Then the particular congressional district used as a case study for this chapter, the Tenth Congressional District of Illinois, is introduced. The two sets of evidence—the publicly recorded donations and the interview data—are then analyzed. These analyses consistently suggest the presence of network effects caused by social pressure.

Political Networks and Contribution Data

As documented beginning with some of the earliest literature in political science, individual political behavior is influenced by social context (Berelson, Lazarsfeld, and McPhee 1954; Putnam 1966; Putnam 2000). In order to measure the impact of donors' social context on their political behavior, it is necessary to identify the donors' political networks.

Political networks are sometimes measured directly through surveys and elsewhere more indirectly through geographic proximity or shared neighborhood, as in the studies described in the previous chapter. Both types of measurements appear to yield substantively significant results. Correlation between an individual's behavior and choices and those of her social network members and political discussants is consistent across network surveys (Huckfeldt and Sprague 1987; Huckfeldt and Sprague 1992; Huckfeldt, Plutzer, and Sprague 1993). Furthermore, spatial correlation in campaign giving has been documented at both a neighborhood and regional level (Cho 2003; Baybeck 2006; Baybeck and Huckfeldt 2002a, 2002b; Cho and Gimpel 2010).

Yet there are possible explanations for geographic correlation in donation patterns that have little to do with social ties. Campaigns target specific groups with shared characteristics. For example, individuals with shared party identification or income may receive similar campaign mailers, or those with shared geographies may receive the same campaign contact from a door-to-door canvassing effort. Particular candidates or organizations may appeal to individuals with certain attributes. Some individuals may simply be more able to contribute to campaigns because of their age, education, or income (Verba, Schlozman, and Brady 1995; Gierzynski 2000; Brown, Powell, and Wilcox 1995; Rosenstone and Hansen 1993). Even after one accounts for shared characteristics, there are likely economies of scale that encourage fundraising efforts to be geographically concentrated. Campaigns will clearly target particular geographies that have developed traditions of campaign contributing (Gerber, Green, and Shachar 2003; Green and Shachar 2000).

Contribution data allow an additional strategy to assess the presence of a political network. Within a fixed geography—such as a single congressional district—it is possible to establish a network variable that weakly parallels the social ties of donors within a district. Two individuals are considered connected in a political network if they have both made a donation to the same organization as documented by public record. This extends the definition of a network tie from that given in the preceding chapter. Individuals are now linked both by geography and by similar behavioral patterns. Codonating individuals are likely to have social ties.

Clearly, not everyone who has made a donation to the same organization will know each other socially. Yet most campaign funds are raised at fundraisers where the donations are elicited through face-to-face contact (Ansolabehere, deFigueiredo, and Snyder 2003; Jones and Hopkins 1985). By focusing analysis on a particular geography as well as within a group of individuals with a shared behavior, it is possible to leverage the importance of both geographic and social connections of donors, many of whom are likely to be located within the same immediate neighborhoods (Huckfeldt and Sprague 1992; Cho 2003; Gimpel, Lee, and Kaminski 2006; Cho and Gimpel 2007). Additionally, campaigns allocate specific resources to identifying social networks in order to leverage these networks to increase donations (Brown, Powell, and Wilcox 1995; Francia et al. 2003). It is likely that there is a social influence component to this giving (Freeman 1997). For social influence to be effective, donors must know each other. A weak measurement of the presence of these social relationships is cogiving.

The Tenth Congressional District of Illinois

The Tenth Congressional District of Illinois was chosen for this analysis not because it is a representative congressional district but specifically because it is unusual. The Tenth Congressional District is unusual in its affluence, strong support for both major political parties, and total number of campaign donations. In the typical congressional district, more than two-thirds of the individual donations come from outside the district boundaries (Gimpel, Lee, and Pearson-Merkowitz 2008). Yet the residents of the Tenth Congressional District are active donors, a fact likely associated with their personal wealth and their frequent exposure to close elections. Gimpel, Lee, and Pearson-Merkowitz (2008) refer to these frequent, wealthy donors as members of the "donor class." The study described here focuses on the social interactions between donors of this type. The ample fundraising activity in this district facilitates the study of social network research, as many of the donors will likely have interacted with each other at district-level fundraisers. By focusing on a congressional district where many residents are members of the "donor class," it is possible to rely upon the geography of the district to establish network connections. It is unlikely that all donors to the Obama campaign across the nation had personal connections to each other. However, within a single congressional district like the Tenth District of Illinois, it is more likely that donors have regular social interactions. These are the kind of relationships that are observed on social networking websites and consist of friends, peers, family, and colleagues. Without explicit data on individuals' social ties, it is necessary to rely upon proxies such as geography to assess social influence. This unusual district permits geography to serve as an appropriate proxy. If there is no evidence of social giving in such a wealthy, politically competitive district, then there is likely to be little support for social giving in other districts where individuals have less frequent interactions as determined by political contributions. Thus in many ways this district

FIGURE 3.2. The Illinois Tenth Congressional District

provides a critical test of the social campaign giving theory in which geography serves as one of the characteristics that describe the residents'
social network.

Located due north of Chicago and bordering Lake Michigan, as seen
in figure 3.2, Illinois's Tenth Congressional District generates high levels
of campaign donations. In 2008, Cook and Lake Counties in the Tenth
District accounted for the most donations in the state, with $97 million
and $17 million in gifts, respectively.[1] High levels of donations are typi-
cally associated with competitive elections, voters who support both
parties, and affluence. According to the American Community Survey
of 2009, the median family income in the Tenth Congressional District
was $92,083, with 27 percent of families earning above $150,000 and
only .6 percent of families in poverty.[2] The area overall has moderate
political beliefs and supports organizations, local candidates, and national candidates for both major parties. Mark Kirk, a Republican with
fiscally conservative and socially liberal views, won this congressional
seat five times (see table 3.1). Yet the district has voted for Democratic
presidential candidates by a significant margin in the last three general
elections. On the Cook Political Report's Partisan Voter Index, the Illinois Tenth Congressional District is D+6, which means that the area

Table 3.1. Congressional Election Results for the Illinois Tenth Congressional District, 1984–2008

Year	Democratic candidate	Percentage of vote	Republican candidate	Percentage of vote
2008	Daniel J. Seals	44.9	Mark S. Kirk	54.1
2006	Daniel J. Seals	44.7	Mark S. Kirk	55.3
2004	Lee Goodman	33.4	Mark S. Kirk	66.6
2002	Henry H. Perritt	29.5	Mark S. Kirk	70.5
2000	Lauren B. Gash	45.9	Mark S. Kirk	54.1
1998	—	0	John E. Porter	100
1996	Philip R. Torf	29.2	John E. Porter	70.8
1994	Andrew M. Krupp	23.5	John E. Porter	76.5
1992	Michael J. Kennedy	32.8	John E. Porter	67.2
1990	Peg McNamara	28.1	John E. Porter	70.7
1988	Eugene F. Friedman	24.0	John E. Porter	76.0
1986	Robert A. Cleland	22.4	John E. Porter	77.6
1984	Ruth C. Braver	23.2	John E. Porter	76.8

on average cast 6 percent more ballots for the Democratic presidential candidates in 2004 and 2008 than the entire United States.[3]

The Tenth Congressional District's geographic concentration of gifts, wealth, and high rates of contribution make it a likely site of social network effects in campaign giving. At first glance, the geographic pattern of the gifts suggests the presence of social network effects. For example, one geographic area, Sheridan Road, produces a large number of donors and donations. Sheridan Road runs north to south along the shore of Lake Michigan with large, gracious, and expensive mansions on each side. Two hundred seventy-nine contributors (or 3 percent of all contributors) in the Tenth Congressional District live on Sheridan Road.[4] Yet these patterns are not sufficient to demonstrate the presence of social network effects, which requires knowledge of individuals' shared characteristics and degree of social connection. These variables are examined in the contribution data as described in the next section.

Describing Campaign Contribution Data

The campaign contribution information comes from Melissa Data, which provided the Federal Election Commission (FEC) individual-level data on campaign contributions to both local and national political organizations for individuals who resided in the Tenth Congressional District and made a minimum contribution to a federal campaign or organization of at least $250.[5] The final database included 33,344 donations totaling $35,650,388, 12,383 unique donors, and 947 recipients. These contributions were made between June 30, 2006, and January 1, 2009.

The campaign contribution information was merged with information from the Illinois voter file, which records name, gender, birth date, and address of each registered voter. First and last name along with zip code were used to match individuals in the campaign contribution database with individuals in the voter file. Approximately 68 percent of the contributors were identified, and 75 percent of the contributions to individuals were successfully attributed to particular individuals, as unidentified contributors gave fewer gifts. Individuals who were not in the voter file, were not matched, or were matched but missing variables in the voter file had the appropriate variables coded as missing. Aggregate-level income data from the 2000 Census based on zip code were merged into the donor file, specifically, the percentage of families earning over $200,000 in each zip code.[6]

The information obtained from Melissa Data, the Illinois voter file, and the US Census provide rich data on campaign contributions. This data set includes all federal contributions, donations made both locally and to other districts. The frequency of gifts ranges substantially. Of the 12,383 unique donors, slightly more than half gave only one gift (6,641 donors). Most donors gave only a few gifts: the mean number of gifts by an individual in Illinois's Tenth Congressional District was 2.7 with a median of 1 and a standard deviation of 4.5. The median gift was $500.[7] Seven hundred and nine of the 1,066 political organizations received 5 or fewer donations, and 844 political organizations received 10 or fewer donations.[8] The 222 political organizations with 11 or more donations received 30,883 gifts, or approximately 93 percent of all the gifts in the district. The 43 political organizations with 100 or more donations received 25,759 gifts, or approximately 73 percent of all the gifts. For the remaining variables, mean voter history is 75 percent, the median is 80 percent, and over 38 percent of matched donors had perfect voter histories of 100 percent. Of the 8,459 contributors that were identified in the voter file, 5,236, or 62 percent, were male, and 3,223, or 38 percent, were female. Between 18 and 100 years old, campaign donors were clustered around a median age of 55 and mean age of 58.4.[9]

As employer and job title are required by the Federal Election Committee when an individual makes a campaign contribution, it is possible to offer a detailed description of contributors' work life. The most donors (1,527 donors, or 12 percent of all donors) replied not employed, while the most donations came from contributors who were retired

(3,871 donations, or 11 percent of all donations) or self-employed (3,680 donations, or 11 percent of all donations). The top five job titles for donors were attorney (1,053 donors, or 9 percent of all donations), president (298 donors, or 2 percent of all donors), executive (288 donors, or 2 percent of all donors), physician (239 donors, or 2 percent of all donors), and consultant (218 donors, or 1 percent of all donors). Among the twenty-five companies with the most donors were law firms, insurance companies, financial services companies, and organizations in the health industry. Only six of these companies were among the top twenty-five employers in the Chicago metropolitan area, which supports a selection mechanism, like social network effects, for causing campaign contribution niches to develop.

The available data allow explicit statistical tests of residents' donation habits. The next section explores whether the empirical patterns in the observational data and survey data support a theory of social giving. Both survey data and publicly available data on giving patterns provide evidence that individuals' political giving is influenced by their social networks. These empirical patterns suggest that individuals are able to assess the role of their social network in motivating their giving behavior correctly. Yet there are other means of establishing evidence of social interaction. Following the statistical analysis, interviews and observations of a small number of elite donors were compiled from the district. Interactions within this small group of donors were described to highlight the types of social processes that motivate donations.

Degree Centrality and Dollars Given

Scholars who study social networks have developed a number of tools to describe the social relationships between individuals. There are two key distinctions in the description of networks: some networks are described by explicit and institutional social relationships, such as records of marriages (Padgett 1993). Other networks are described by implicit social ties—records of common or shared behaviors like voting patterns (Fowler 2006b). Here, I will use the second method, where individuals are considered to be "linked" to each other in a social network if they have donated to the same organization. The number of organizations to which both donors have contributed represents the strength of their social network tie. Repeating this calculation for all donors establishes an implicit social network.

Scholars are increasingly relying upon objective information to establish social networks. Whether the data consist of cosponsorships

(Fowler 2006), committee assignments in Congress (Porter et al. 2005), or scientific collaborations (Newman 2001), there are clear advantages to using an objective data set to define a social network. There are no problems related to survey nonresponse or recollection. All potential respondents are already included in the observed data. The data that are observed are based upon actual choices and decisions.

This social network, based upon shared donations, is a proxy for the true underlying social relationships. Individuals may have donated to the same organization but never have met; they may, for example, simply share the same set of characteristics and thus had been targeted by these organizations as likely donors. Data from interviews with these donors, however, indicate that many of the codonors are socially connected. That individuals may be less connected than this variable would indicate is not necessarily problematic in the analysis of these data; results based upon this variable would likely be stronger if it were possible to observe true social connections.

Using codonation as a definition of connectedness, it is then possible to establish each individual's *degree centrality* in the donor network. Centrality is a measurement of the relative importance of each individual within the network. Recall that each individual is connected to each other individual if they have both donated to the same organization. The more frequently the pair of individuals donate to the same organizations, the stronger their connection. Suppose two individuals both donated to eight common organizations. The strength of their network tie would then be eight. A central actor in the donation network will then have made numerous donations to the same organizations as many other individuals. *Degree centrality* is defined as the sum of these connections across all individuals in the network (Freeman 1977, 1979). Suppose an individual made many gifts to popular organizations—organizations to which many other people also contributed. This individual would have a high degree centrality. In contrast, suppose an individual made many gifts to organizations to which no on else contributed. This individual would have a low degree centrality. This measurement is intended to capture the social aspect of giving. Individuals who give to organizations that are shared within the network are more likely to have their gifts observed by others. In figure 3.3, the two graphs provide examples of individuals with high and low degree centrality. Suppose the individuals represented by both gray nodes made four political contributions each. In the top left figure, the gray node has four connections with the other individuals in the graph. This represents having made donations to organizations to which the other four nodes had also contributed. In

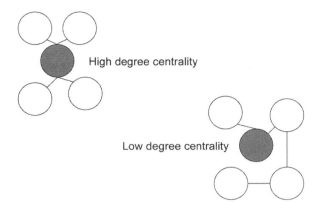

FIGURE 3.3. Example of degree centrality

Suppose the individual represented by each gray node made four contributions. The top left gray node represents a person who donated to four organizations also donated to by individuals represented by each of the white nodes. The bottom right gray node represents a person who donated to two organizations also donated to by individuals represented by two white nodes. The gray node in each graph depicts a different level of degree centrality. The top left node has high degree centrality (4), whereas the bottom right node has low degree centrality (2). Note that the person represented by the bottom right gray node also does not have the highest degree centrality in her graph, as one person represented by a white node also donated to two organizations shared by two other white nodes.

the bottom right figure, the gray node has two connections. This would represent having made donations to organizations to which the top two nodes had also contributed. No one else made donations to two other organizations represented in this graph. The presence of other links between nodes other than the gray node indicate that the other nodes had contributed but to different organizations than those to which the gray node had contributed. The top left gray node is thus more central in her network.

If there is a social component of giving, then individuals with high degree centrality should donate larger amounts. That is, increasing the social visibility of an individual's giving patterns should stimulate additional giving. It is not possible to separate who is socially connected from who donates to the same organizations in the donation data. To remedy this, the donation data are used to generate the degree centrality variable. Suppose that an individual had donated to four organizations to which other individuals in the district had also donated, as illustrated by the top left graph in figure 3.2. That individual probably would not personally know all four of those other individuals—they might have had dinner together at campaign events for years, they might be personal friends, or they might have each made online donations to the campaigns without having ever met. That is, codonating is a weak proxy for social connectedness. Any empirical support to suggest that this variable generates additional campaign giving is likely an underestimate of the true social network effect.

Such an estimate is observed in figure 3.4, where the individual donor's degree centrality is plotted on the *x*-axis and the total dollar amount of all gifts is plotted on the *y*-axis. A linear regression line is plotted between the two.[10] There is a slight positive relationship between degree and total dollars contributed. As more congressional district residents give to the same organizations, donors contribute more dollars to those organizations. If we assume that degree centrality is associated with personal connections, then this figure suggests that as the gift becomes more publicly visible—that is, as the degree centrality of the donor increases—the donor becomes more likely to contribute more total dollars in campaign donations.

The hypothesis tested is that the total amount of money donated is a function of degree centrality, controlled for total number of gifts and a variety of other covariates that are likely to determine the total dollars donated. If degree centrality has the expected effect, then as degree centrality increases, an individual should be more likely to donate additional dollars. The total number of gifts is necessary as a control variable

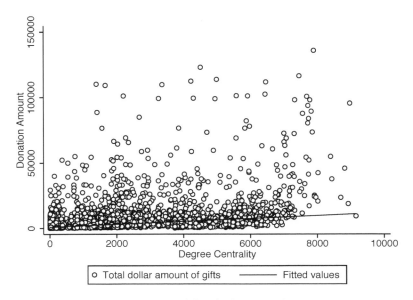

FIGURE 3.4. Total donation amount (in dollars) by degree centrality

to ensure that it isn't simply the case that individuals with high degree centrality—who have made a sufficiently large number of donations to have high degree centrality—donate large dollar amounts. Controlling for the total number of gifts ensures that the effect of the degree centrality variable will reveal the marginal rate of increased dollars donated as a function of the social component of campaign giving. It is also necessary to include the control variables that are typically associated with campaign donations, particularly income, gender, and age.

In a negative binomial regression, where the dependent variable is the total dollars donated and the independent variables include degree centrality, total number of gifts, the percentage of households in the zip code with incomes over $200,000, gender, and age, degree centrality has a positive and statistically significant coefficient.[11] In terms of the magnitude of this effect, changing the degree centrality from the smallest value observed in the data to the largest value observed in the data would result in an increased rate of donation of $546.42. Coefficients from this regression and first differences without the covariates are included in table 3.2. The percentage of families in the zip code with incomes over $200,000 is positively associated with increased donations, as expected. Age is associated with fewer donations.

This is an extremely small but positive effect of degree. These results strongly suggest that there is a social effect of campaign giving. They correspond to the theoretical explanation of social influence: that public visibility of a particular behavior, within a social network where the behavior is a social norm, increases the frequency of the behavior.

Table 3.2. Negative Binomial Regression Coefficients: Effect of Degree on Dollars Given

Variable	Coefficient with covariates	Coefficient without covariates
Degree	.00003* (.00000)	.00002* (.00000)
Total number of gifts	.22589* (.00461)	.24628* (.00401)
Percentage of families over $200K	.01751* (.00081)	
Female	−.05343 (.02153)	
Age	−.00554* (.00082)	
Constant	6.6719* (.05183)	6.8267* (.01419)
N	8,244	12,383
Pseudo R2	.0456	.0409
First differences (min. to max. degree)	$546.42 (131.21)	$275.65 (97.38)

Note: The difference in the number of observations reflects the presence of missing data in the covariates in the first column. These results are robust to the exclusion of the two outliers (individuals who made more than one hundred gifts), replacement of the census variable for income with data that approximate each individual's current home value (from the website Zillow), and fixed effects for each campaign or organization. Standard errors are shown in parentheses.
* $\alpha = .05$.

In this case, everyone in this network contributes to campaigns. It is already established as a social norm. Those whose behavior is the most observed by others in the district are likely to contribute the most total dollars. To ascertain their motivations for donating, these contributors were surveyed, as described in the next section.

Donor Relationships

To further support the FEC donation data and subsequent personal interviews, 1,000 individual surveys were mailed to randomly selected donors in the Tenth Congressional District, with 220 completed and returned. These surveys contained six questions. Responses to the first question listed the names of seventy-five other district residents and asked donors to circle the names of individuals whom they had met at least once.[12] One-third of these names were those of the top donors in the district. One-third of these names were randomly selected from possible condonors, that is, individuals who had given to the same political organizations and campaigns as the respondent. One-third of these names were randomly selected from donors who were also residents of the district but had contributed to different organizations than the respondent.

This survey question allows a test of the idea that donations are social. If donors know their codonors more frequently than they know donors in the district who have donated to different organizations, then there is support for using codonation as a proxy variable for social relationships. Additionally, this is evidence that there are social relationships within the donor pool. Of the 159 individuals who respondent to the survey, very few respondents were able to identify many names. Respondents knew an average of .27 donors to different organizations (min. 0, max. 3), 1.05 codonors (min. 0, max. 23), and 1.14 top donors (min. 0, max. 11). The ordering of these averages, though, is consistent with the theory that there are more personal relationships among codonors. A t-test confirms that the average number of relationships with codonors is statistically significantly larger than the average number of relationships with other donors ($t = 3.67$).

Respondents also knew a relatively large number of the top donors, but the rate at which they knew the top donors is not statistically distinct from the rate at which they knew their codonors. That the top donors have obtained such prominence in the district again suggests the mechanism that motivates political contributions—the top donors have strong social relationships with other donors. This is a necessary (albeit not sufficient) step toward demonstrating that a component of campaign giving is attributable to a social norm.

How often individuals recognized these names provides a critical test of the hypothesis that codonation patterns are social—a necessary condition for social giving is that individuals recognize the names of their codonors. Furthermore, it is possible to use these survey data to establish a donor social network that is distinct from codonations. Below, methods of doing so are explored.

First, it is possible to use the total number of individuals whom each survey respondent identified to predict the total amount of donations. If donations are driven by social influence, then individuals with a larger social network should donate more (Shang and Croson 2009). Repeating the negative binomial regression described previously predicts the total amount of gifts as a function of each survey respondent's network size. Table 3.3 shows these results, where each individual's network size is a positive but not significant predictor of the total amount given, controlling for income, age, gender, and the total number of gifts contributed.[13]

Second, it is possible to use the date of the donation to determine whether donation patterns are consistent with a social explanation. The FEC indicates the date when each individual made a contribution.[14] This allows us to compare the time difference between the donations made by individuals who are not identified as social network members with the time between donations made by individuals who are identified

Table 3.3. Negative Binomial Regression Coefficients: Effect of Network Size on Dollars Given

Variable	Coefficient with covariates	Coefficient without covariates
Network size	.036 (.020)	.026 (.020)
Total number of gifts	.223* (.019)	.225* (.021)
Percentage of families over $200K		.011* (.005)
Female		.177 (.177)
Age		−.001 (.005)
Constant	6.40* (.098)	6.08* (.342)
N	220	211
First differences (min. to max. network size)	$1,099.54 (747.54)	$749.89 (652.29)

Note: The difference in the number of observations reflects the presence of missing data in the covariates in the first column. The sample includes all individuals who responded to the mail survey asking them to identify up to seventy-five individuals from the congressional district whom they had met "at least once." Standard errors are shown in parentheses.
* α = .05.

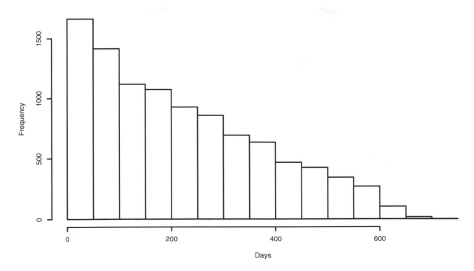

FIGURE 3.5. Days between gifts, all donors
   Mean number of days: 218.89, standard deviation 162.89. The histogram represents the distribution of the total number of days between gifts obtained by randomly drawing gifts made by ten thousand pairs of individuals from the pool of donors and comparing the time between those gifts.

as social network members. This tests the hypothesis that if network members influence each other, then they should give gifts more closely timed than the rest of the donors in the congressional district.

In order to compare the time between gifts by networked and non-networked donors, two gifts made by two different individuals in the donor data set were randomly selected. The number of days between their gifts was calculated, and this process was repeated ten thousand times. For comparison, two gifts made by different individuals identified from the survey as social network members (where one individual identifies the other as someone she has met at least once) were then randomly selected. Again, the number of days between their gifts was calculated, and this process was repeated ten thousand times. The resulting histograms are illustrated in figures 3.5 and 3.6.

Those individuals identified in the survey as members of a common social network made donations more closely timed together: the mean number of days between two randomly selected donors is 218.89, whereas the mean number of days between two randomly selected networked donors is 199.86. Individuals who knew each other gave gifts that were approximately two weeks closer together on average than those who did not. A t-test to compare the means of these distributions

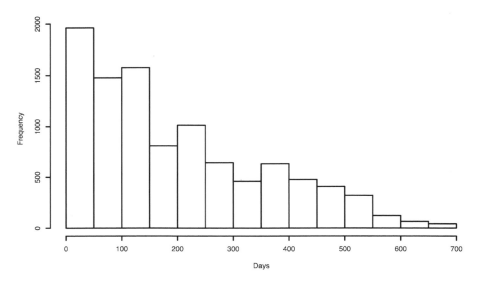

FIGURE 3.6. Days between gifts, networked donors
   Mean number of days: 199.86, standard deviation 155.84. The histogram represents the distribution of the total number of days between gifts obtained by randomly drawing gifts made by ten
thousand pairs of individuals from the pool of networked donors and comparing the time between
those gifts.

yields a t-statistic of 8.36—a statistically distinguishable value. One
possibility is that this is attributable to the fact that they also gave
to the same organizations, so the analysis is repeated but instead by
drawing the comparison for the time between gifts across networked
codonors and nonnetworked codonors. This comparison yields similar
results: the mean number of days between gifts made by two randomly
selected codonors is 204.38, whereas the mean number of days between
gifts made by two randomly selected networked codonors is 196.87
(t-statistic for difference-in-means test is 8.36).

The remaining survey questions address whether particular groups
associated with the respondent also donate: family, friends, neighbors,
and extended family. In these data, 65.41 percent of the respondents
indicated that their immediate family also contributed to political campaigns, 66.04 percent indicated that their friends also contribute to
political campaigns, 27.67 percent indicated that their neighbors also
contribute to political campaigns, and 37 percent indicated that their
extended family also contribute to political campaigns. High correlation
in giving patterns among the closer relationships (friends and family)
and weaker correlation in giving patterns among the more distant rela-

tionships (neighbors and extended family) also support a mechanism of social influence, wherein there should be larger effects (and hence larger correlations) in closer relationships.

In summary, these survey data confirm that social relationships do exist between codonors and that many of the donors belong to family and friendship networks with a norm of campaign giving. Two themes consistent with these results emerge in the responses to open-ended survey questions. The first is that individual donors contribute based upon a desire to support particular candidates. When asked to describe why they make campaign contributions, individuals consistently identified the desire to intervene with particular campaigns and candidates. Figure 3.7 illustrates the most frequent words used in these open-ended responses.[15] Recall that every individual in this data set has made contributions.

Yet there is significance evidence of social influence as well. Donors believe they have successfully influenced other individuals to make contributions. When asked to identify whom they have influenced, individuals most commonly reported that they had successfully persuaded their friends and family to contribute. Figure 3.8 illustrates the most frequent words used in these open-ended responses.[16]

That these individuals believe they have been successful at influencing their family and friends is distinctly possible given the other empirical results, which large support a narrative that social influence plays a significant role in campaign contribution decisions. This evidence ac-

FIGURE 3.7. Frequent words in responses to the open-ended survey question "Please describe why you make campaign contributions"

FIGURE 3.8. Frequent words in responses to the open-ended survey question "Whom have you influenced and how have you done so?"

cords with some early evidence from the ANES. In 1964, respondents were asked whether they gave to campaigns and how they were solicited. The proportion of those solicited by mail who gave was 25.2 percent, and the proportion of those solicited by telephone who gave was 28.6 percent. This is in stark contrast to the proportion of those solicited face-to-face who gave, which was 62.8 percent.

Wednesday Morning Coffee

One Wednesday morning each month in the Tenth Congressional District, a group of women gather for coffee. They are old friends. They have lived in the district for many years. They talk to each other about the local schools, about the weather, and about their neighborhood. They mostly come to talk about politics. These women are all influential Democratic political donors in their district. Early in the primary election season, they invite Democratic candidates to these Wednesday morning coffees to speak about both their ideological platforms and their personal autobiographies. These women debate with each other about which candidate they want to support. They decide. Together, they then go out and campaign, convincing other friends and family to contribute to these candidates and causes. They host open houses for the candidates and leave personal notes of invitation for their neighbors to attend and make a small campaign contribution. They recruit personal friends to attend campaign events and fundraisers, sometimes even covering the cost of admission in order to persuade another supporter. These women are the political leaders of the district, and their relationship with each other is both political and personal. This is a prime example of a political network.

In the Democratic congressional primary in the Tenth Congressional District, Dan Seals was running for Congress for the third time. In his two previous campaigns (in 2006 and 2008) he had been the Democratic nominee for the district but had been unable to beat Mark Kirk. The women of the coffee group had been strong supporters of Seals. Several of them had hosted events in their homes during his previous campaigns. They had introduced Seals to their friends. They felt personally invested in his campaign.

Yet in the primary campaign in 2010, not all of the group members were necessarily confident that Seals was the right candidate for the district. He had failed to win in two previous attempts. Should these women support his third try? Some suggested that perhaps it was time for a new Democratic challenger. Others disagreed. Finally, one Wednesday, the other tenable Democratic primary candidate, Julie Hamos, was invited to the Wednesday coffee. Hamos was currently serving as a member of the Illinois House of Representatives, and her district—the Eighteenth District—overlapped with much of the Tenth Congressional District. She had been in public office since 1999 and appeared to be a viable candidate.

After Hamos spoke about her congressional candidacy, the hostess of the Wednesday coffee thanked her for her time. The hostess then turned to the coffee group and asked, "Will you please take out your checkbooks?" With the split opinion in the group about support for Seals and Hamos, many of the women at the coffee were conflicted. Should they support the same candidate as their friend, the coffee hostess, even though they liked that candidate less than Seals?

Many women at the coffee that day wrote checks, and several of them indicated a level of discomfort with doing so. Campaign giving patterns are significantly influenced by friends, as this story illustrates. The outcome of this anecdote is reflected in interview data that demonstrate a social basis of campaign giving. Noted social psychologist

Robert Cialdini describes "weapons of influence" used by the Tupperware company to increase home sales of their product. Hostesses of these events invite a salesperson from the Tupperware company to her house, along with a number of her friends. The Tupperware salesperson and the hostess split the proceeds of the party. At each Tupperware party there is reciprocity (each person receives a gift), public commitment (each participant describes the benefits and uses of the Tupperware she already owns), and social proof (the sheet to order the new Tupperware is passed around the room). Cialdini notes that this is a ferociously successful business strategy—Tupperware sales exceed $2.5 million per day (Cialdini 2007). The Wednesday morning coffees described above—and the donations made to Hamos by previous Seals supporters—are consistent with the same kind of psychological mechanisms that have made Tupperware parties successful. Individuals have a difficult time resisting appeals by their friends. The coffee hostess produced reciprocity (she served coffee), public commitment (participants talked about their support of Hamos), and social proof (she asked her guests to take out their checkbooks). It is difficult to refuse a friend with whom there is a personal connection, someone known and liked. It is not surprising that many women who attended the Wednesday morning coffee wrote checks to Hamos.

The empirical results described above reflect the findings of interviews conducted with major donors in the Tenth Congressional District. Twenty-one individuals who are both donors and residents of the Tenth Congressional District were independently interviewed in an effort to ascertain their actual motivations in contributing. The respondents were asked a series of open-ended questions about their motivations for contributing to campaigns. Interview data are complicated to interpret. On one hand, asking people questions about whom they know or their giving patterns is likely to elicit sincere, detailed answers. On the other hand, asking people questions about why they contributed to a particular campaign requires the respondents to report on the existence of particular stimuli or an inferential process, known problematic features of interview data (Nisbett and Wilson 1977). With that caveat in mind, it is useful to at least compare the interview narratives with the empirical results as a potential way to illustrate the mechanism driving the empirical patterns.

Three central themes emerge from these interviews. First, individuals report being influenced by their social network members to contribute. Nine of the twenty-one interviewees reported being influenced by their friends and family in a variety of ways. Said one respondent, "Lately, I have only given out of obligation—or my sense thereof—to a friend or associate from whom I solicited funds for Obama." Another reported that "my last contribution was influenced by the emails from my political friends who were all grappling with the same decision."

Second, the respondents reported leveraging their social ties to get additional donations for the organizations they support. Twelve of the twenty-one respondents reported influencing individuals around them to contribute. Said one respondent, "I had significant influence on my immediate friends. Anyone who wanted to talk politics, I would ask if they had contributed, and I would say, 'You can't complain to me until you've written a check.' " In particular, individuals reported leveraging their family connections. Husbands, wives, and children were most frequently identified as individuals whom the respondent had strongly encouraged to donate money. Parents particularly described their pride when their children had begun to contribute, as a sign that they had finally matured and realized the need for them to participate in politics in this particular way. Said one donor, "I go door-to-door and leave personal notes for the neighbors. I ask people to participate for free. It's why I invite people as my guest. My original invitation to participate was from a friend—she realized that she wasn't just one person but that she could do something." These individual descriptions of how donors have influenced their families, neighbors, and friends to participate support the hypothesis that strong social ties are key to maintaining social norms of political behavior.

Third, individuals identified campaign giving with social relationships. Sixteen out of twenty-one donors indicated that their families donate to campaigns. Nineteen out of twenty-one donors indicated that their friends contributed. Thirteen of the twenty-one donors indicated that their neighbors donated, and nine of the twenty-one donors indicated that their extended family donated. Close social ties are associated with similar giving patterns. Anecdotally, these donors report being more likely to attend fundraisers if there are names they recognize in the "invite heading." They also report inviting their own friends to attend these events with them and that fundraising events are places to socialize but also to demonstrate social status. Said one donor, "There's a social benefit to go to fundraisers—a lot of good friends go and it is nice to be with people who share my core beliefs." Said another, "I will also bring someone to the fundraisers as my guest and encourage them to give via an open-ended request, whatever they can and want, as a little gets them committed." These reports correspond with social giving that helps to maintain a norm of participation but also to maintain group membership.

It Matters Whose Name Is on the Invitation

Using a single congressional district as a case study, this chapter illustrates how campaign giving is frequently driven by social influence. The political behavior exhibited by the residents of this district suggests that donating, like voting, is sustained by a desire to adhere to the social norms of a social network. Derived from a variety of methods, from interviewing residents to investigating patterns in observational data, the evidence in this chapter consistently supports a theory of social giving.

The advantage of focusing on a single case study is that it is possible to investigate an entire social network to look for consistency in the evidence that social ties motivate donations. The disadvantage is the loss of generalizability, in the sense that the congressional district chosen as a case for this chapter is not representative of the typical congressional district in the United States. Yet as the Obama campaign webpage anecdote illustrates, there are likely fundamental aspects of human sociability that are expressed through campaign giving regardless of the avenue by which donating takes place. While other chapters in this book look at data drawn from a national probability sample, this chapter focuses narrowly on one set of donors to illustrate the mechanisms that persuade them to donate to political campaigns and organizations.

The in-person interviews generated consistent reports of donors influencing others to contribute and often identified particular strategies, including sending e-mails to friends about donating and inviting friends to events. The primary theme in these strategies is that of leveraging a social tie to take political action. Donating to political campaigns is part of the social norm for certain groups of individuals. The types of individuals who are solicited and the reports of participation correspond with the theory that the primary mechanism that allows individuals to influence others to donate is that of maintaining personal relationships by adhering to the social norms held by social network ties. These social norms are expressed via social pressure. Close family ties stimulate donations. Personal connections matter most. For example, one respondent explained that by door-to-door canvassing and leaving personal notes for her neighbors, she had been able to increase the attendance at fundraisers. Participating in fundraising is a personal act. An invitation to attend a coffee for Dan Seals, the Democratic congressional candidate whose repeat candidacy generated tension at the Wednesday morning coffee, is shown in figure 3.9.

Note that the invitation lists the full names of a number of individuals who have clearly donated at the highest level possible. This sets up

DAN SEALS
DEMOCRAT FOR CONGRESS

Please Join

Joan & Julian Berman, Bill Crowley, Paige & Joe Dooley
Jean & Dick Doub, Karen Fujisawa & Carl Robinson
Kit & Steve Harper, Ruth Krugly & Darryl Davidson
Anne & Russ Mayerfeld, Marcia & Jack Melamed
Cathy & Jim Nowacki, Nancy Pred & Wade Thoma
Priscilla & Fred Sperling, Peggy & Paul Slater
Mary Stowell & Jim Streicker, Annette Turow
Jane Weintraub & Clark Ellithorpe, Ann S. Wolff
Host Committee in formation

and

Dan Seals

Democrat for U.S. Congress (IL-10)
Tuesday, September 22, 2009
7:00-8:30 pm
at the home of Mary Stowell & Jim Streicker
301 Woodley Road
Winnetka, Illinois

Suggested Contributions:
$1000 - Host
$500 - Sponsor
$150 - Patron

To RSVP or for more information, please contact Mimi Rodman at 847.945.8900 or by email at
mrodman@dansealsforcongress.com. Contributions made in advance or in lieu of attending may be sent
in the enclosed envelope or by visiting www.dansealsforcongress.com/contribute.php.

Contributions or gifts to Dan Seals for Congress are not tax deductible. Federal law requires us to use our
best efforts to collect and report the name, mailing address, occupation and name of employer of individuals
whose contributions exceed $200 in an election cycle. Contributions to Dan Seals for Congress are subject
to the prohibitions and limitations of the Federal Election Campaign Act. That law prohibits contributions
from corporations, labor unions, national banks, government contractors and foreign nationals who are
not entitled to permanent residence. All contributions must be made from personal funds and may not be
reimbursed by any other person.

www.DanSealsforCongress.com

PAID FOR BY DAN SEALS FOR CONGRESS

FIGURE 3.9. Example of Dan Seals's campaign donation invitation

a social norm of giving for the recipients of this mailer: expected guests (whom potential attendees may be likely to know) are listed, and 'Suggested Contributions' are encouraged. Because people whom the recipients are likely to know are listed, the recipients realize that their friends also expect them to follow their giving behavior. In the randomized field experiments involving National Public Radio (Shang and Croson 2010; Shang, Croson, and Reed 2010) and the college alumni fund (Frey and Meier 2004), it was clear that signaling social norm expectations of fellow social network members generates donations. The Seals coffee invitation mailer does exactly the same thing.

The interview findings correspond with the patterns in the aggregate data for this congressional district—the dollar amount donated increased with respect to degree centrality when controlled for total donations and other factors likely to affect donation amounts. The coefficient on the degree centrality variable is small but statistically significant and positive, which supports the hypothesis that if individuals are more likely to be observed in their behavior, they will donate additional dollars. These regressions indicate that degree centrality can affect donation choices. Survey data support using degree centrality as a proxy for the visibility of the gift and further indicate that respondents are frequently embedded in family and friend networks that also donate to campaigns.

The empirical results and the survey data demonstrate the effects of social pressure. The advantage of analyzing patterns in donation data as opposed to using geography as a network proxy is that individuals are likely to know codonors in a way in which they are less likely to know their physical neighbors.

The dollar amount of individual contributions to political organizations, controlled for a range of other factors, is directly related to the number of shared organizations to which an individual's social network members contribute. When the number of donor organizations shared among givers increases, individuals contribute more total dollars, controlled for the rate of giving. This pattern of behavior is attributable to social influence. These empirical results on donating contribute to the body of evidence that political behavior has a social foundation. The donation patterns suggest that some part of giving is attributable to a shared social action. That is, the donors appear to know and influence each other, the donors' friends and families are also contributors, and as the donation becomes more publicly visible, individuals give more total dollars. Yet these data do little to control for the problems of homophily, whereby individuals form social connections to other individuals with whom they share characteristics. Likely many donors have become friends because of their personal wealth, and wealth is also highly associated with campaign donations. Therefore, while this empirical evidence is consistent with the theory that political behaviors are social, it does not provide causal evidence. That these results are consistent with other types of social donation experiments, however, and that the results of the observational, interview, and survey data align illustrate the social influence mechanism. Donating appears to be based on social norms and social networks.

The success of online fundraising is intrinsically linked to making donations increasingly publicly visible. The Obama online campaign dramatically highlighted the role of personal networks in political behavior and allowed individuals to participate in politics as part of their regular social interactions. According to the campaign website, "Two weeks after Election Day, supporters are continuing to use the online tools at 'My.BarackObama.com.' " Individuals developed political relationships within their preexisting social relationships. These social relationships did not end on Election Day, resulting in continued website use despite the fact that the political campaign had ended. As seen in the snapshot of the My.BarackObama.com page shown in figures 3.10 and 3.11, supporters are asked to "invite your friends and family to join the network" and to "set a fundraising goal, invite your friends, and track your progress." A conspicuous aspect of the My.Barack.Obama.com webpage is its emphasis on participation through social ties. This emphasis does not so much encourage exchange of information as it encourages establishing a social norm of contributing to political campaigns. According to Joe Trippi, Howard Dean's 2004 campaign advisor, "Ever since the TV era began in 1960, every single presidential campaign in America has been top-down. Only two have been bottom-up. One was Dean. The other is Obama" (Berman 2008). The bottom-up Obama campaign relied upon a social network of political donors.

The decision to participate in politics by donating money to campaigns is very publicly observable—records are publicly available online regarding each individual's contributions, and friends are likely to notice the presence of other friends at campaign events and fundraisers. Therefore, this is a political behavior that is likely to be significantly affected by social networks. Donors to campaigns are not typical citizens.[17] They are "overwhelmingly rich and well-educated" (Francia et al. 2003, 27). Donors are also disproportionately likely to participate in other political behaviors as well—voting, attending meetings, writing letters, and talking to others about politics (Rosenstone and Hansen 1993; Verba,

"I'M ASKING YOU TO BELIEVE.
Not just in my ability to bring about
real change in Washington ... I'm
asking you to believe in yours."

Betsy Sinclair

Logout | Account/Password

MY PROFILE   Edit Profile

Share some basic information about yourself and why you support Barack Obama.
Create Your Profile

NEIGHBOR TO NEIGHBOR
CAMPAIGNS AVAILABLE TO YOU

Georgia Phone Campaign   Get Started
Voters Available
Get out the vote for Jim Martin for US Senate to help Barack Obama implement his vision in Washington, DC!

Also, to organize a...

MY BLOG   Manage Blog

Share your thoughts and experiences with other Obama supporters. Whether it's a photo, personal story, or simply your opinion on the campaign, you can share it through a personal blog.
Manage Your Blog

MAKING A DIFFERENCE   What's This?

MY ACTIVITIES

1

	All 7 Days 30 Days	
My Activity Index Details	Events Hosted	0
	Events Attended	0
	Calls made	0
	Doors Knocked	0
	Number of blog posts	0
	Donors to your personal fundraising	0
	Amount raised	$0.00
	Groups Joined	0

FACEBOOK

Connect your Facebook account to your MyBO Account

f Connect with Facebook

ANNOUNCEMENTS

Share your ideas to help shape the future of this movement

Your hard work built this movement. Now it's up to you to decide how we move forward:

Share your campaign experience and your thoughts on the best way to keep supporting our agenda for change.

This Victory Is Yours

Thank you for everything you have done to help this campaign. Because of the work you did, Barack Obama has been elected

My Home

Community
My Neighborhood
My Groups
My Friends
Find Friends

Events
Find Events
Host an Event
Manage my Events

Contact voters

Fundraising

Messages

Blog
View All Blogs
Search All Blogs

Action Center

Resources

FIGURE 3.10. My.BarackObama.com member profile, page 1

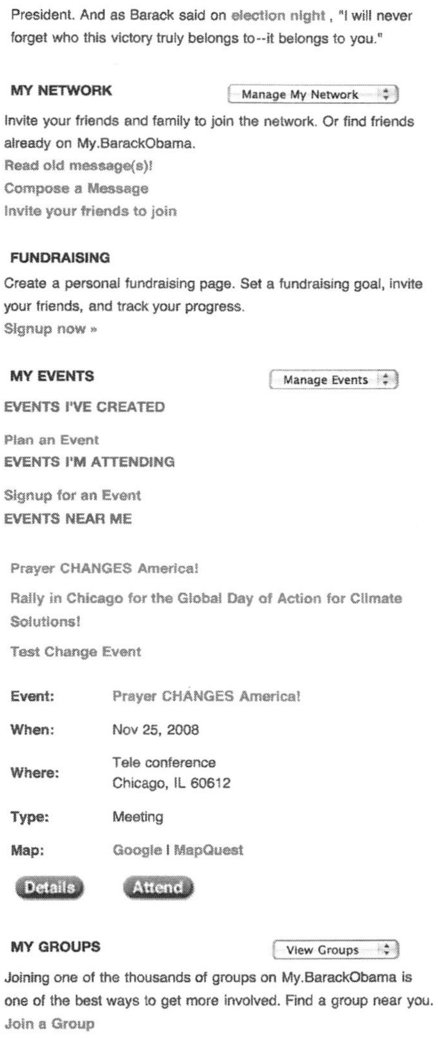

President. And as Barack said on election night , "I will never forget who this victory truly belongs to--it belongs to you."

MY NETWORK   [Manage My Network ⬍]

Invite your friends and family to join the network. Or find friends already on My.BarackObama.
Read old message(s)!
Compose a Message
Invite your friends to join

FUNDRAISING

Create a personal fundraising page. Set a fundraising goal, invite your friends, and track your progress.
Signup now »

MY EVENTS   [Manage Events ⬍]

EVENTS I'VE CREATED

Plan an Event
EVENTS I'M ATTENDING

Signup for an Event
EVENTS NEAR ME

Prayer CHANGES America!

Rally in Chicago for the Global Day of Action for Climate Solutions!

Test Change Event

Event:	Prayer CHANGES America!
When:	Nov 25, 2008
Where:	Tele conference Chicago, IL 60612
Type:	Meeting
Map:	Google I MapQuest

(Details)   (Attend)

MY GROUPS   [View Groups ⬍]

Joining one of the thousands of groups on My.BarackObama is one of the best ways to get more involved. Find a group near you.
Join a Group

FIGURE 3.11. My.BarackObama.com member profile, page 2

Schlozman, and Brady 1995). Donors contribute based upon their partisanship, interests, ideology, and personal identity (Francia et al. 2003; Mansbridge 2003). These characteristics are frequently associated with many types of political participation. Political participation often poses a collective action problem in traditional political science, and the suggestion here is that the collective action problem is resolved by a network effect. Reciprocity, reputation, and simply making the behavior publicly visible are all mechanisms susceptible to social contagion. The fact that these political elites are subject to the same types of social influence in their donation participation as average citizens are influenced by in their voting participation in South Los Angeles suggests that our political behaviors are social and that this phenomenon is a common part of the fabric of our human experience.

What do these results indicate about the social citizen? The empirical work implies that as gifts are more public, there is increased pressure to adhere to a social norm of giving. As appears to be generally the case with political participation, most people are inclined to participate in politics because someone asked them to do so (Brady, Schlozman, and Verba 1999). The social citizen donates money to campaigns—or makes additional donations—when someone from her social network notices the gift. These are public acts of adherence to a social norm of giving. Casting a ballot is also maintained by a social norm. The chapters that follow explore the extent to which choice, as opposed to participation, is also affected by social networks and social norms.

4

Candidate Choice: What Makes a Democrat Vote like a Republican?

What makes a Democrat vote for a Republican candidate? To what extent can an individual's social context affect her vote choice? For example, suppose an individual moved from St. George, Utah, to Santa Monica, California. St. George, Utah, is one of the most conservative cities in the United States. Over 90 percent of the population in St. George, Utah, is white, 63 percent of all households are married couples, and over 80 percent of voters cast their presidential vote for George W. Bush in November 2000. Santa Monica, California, is one of the most liberal cities in the United States. Not only is the Santa Monica mayor a member of the Green Party, but in November 2000 approximately 80 percent of the voters in Santa Monica cast their ballots for Al Gore. If a voter were to move from St. George to Santa Monica, the political preferences of her social group would likely change, in particular if she chose her social group based upon shared characteristics (presence of children, income, race, age, marital status) and not based upon politics. Social group politics have the potential to influence an individual's politics to an extent that a move such as the one described above can change an individual's vote choice.

The 2000 ANES reveals that quite a number of liberals vote for Republican candidates and vice versa. According to respondents' reported vote choice for president and ideological self-placement, 11 percent of self-identified liberals voted for the Republican presidential candidate, and 29 percent of self-identified conservatives voted for the Democratic presidential candidate in the 2000 ANES.[1] What are the motivations for these ideologues to switch their votes from their political predispositions? This chapter explores the possibility that the voter's calculus incorporates contextual factors, such as influence from their social network.

Two Studies of Social Network Voting: Gore and Obama

Partisan political discussion networks have consequences for an individual's presidential vote choice in two distinct cases explored through survey data sets in this chapter. Each survey asked respondents to describe their own candidate preferences along with their socioeconomic and demographic characteristics and solicited a political network of up to three discussants. The discussants' partisan preferences are used as the independent variable in subsequent analysis, where the respondent is subject to influence from these discussants. Analysis of the two surveys requires different sets of assumptions in order to draw causal inferences. If a series of assumptions about the data-generating processes are accepted, however, political networks play highly influential roles in determining an individual's candidate choice in both sets of analyses.

The first study uses the 2000 ANES to determine whether reported political discussants' presidential choices influence the respondent's presidential vote choice. These data provide the survey respondent's partisan breakdown of her discussion network and locates the respondent within a particular congressional district. The partisanship of the respondent's discussion network and congressional district affect the respondent's presidential vote choice. The data include a large number of covariates that alleviate biases introduced by the respondent's selection of particular discussants based upon their shared characteristics. Even with those covariates included as control variables, there are statistically significant discussion network effects on the respondent's presidential vote choice. That is, when we control for political ideology and other relevant covariates, we find that the politics of a voter's social context influences her voting behavior. Furthermore, the network effect is robust to model specification. There is a visible contextual effect on vote choice regardless of political or demographic similarities between respondents. A simple logit analysis indicates that the contextual variables add explanatory power to the traditional calculus of voting model.

Yet individuals may influence as well as be influenced by discussants. Unless a particular structure for influence is assumed, solicitation of discussants' political preferences in a single time period can only provide correlations with the respondent's preferences.[2] This problem may be resolved through analysis of panel data. Analysis of panel data allows for changes in ideology, candidate preference, and party identification for both the respondent and the discussants.

The second study uses a panel data set generated through an Internet survey, the Cooperative Campaign Analysis Project (CCAP), conducted in January, October, and November 2008. The respondents were asked to provide information about themselves in each panel and about their political discussants in both October and November. This allows differences over time to be leveraged in order to identify the effect of discussant preferences on an individual's level of support for the major presidential candidates. When the selection of the social context in terms of political ideology and other relevant covariates are controlled for, a voter's choice of candidate is influenced by the political preferences of her social network. This analysis determines the existence of social network effects after controlling for the selection of social networks. Both the partisanship of the respondent's discussion network and intended vote preferences are observed to have an effect on the respondent's presidential vote choice, support for particular candidates, and change in support. This allows observation of network effects on vote choice regardless of political or demographic similarities between network members. This work extends the first study's survey data results to demonstrate that discussants can influence political choices.

This data discussed in this chapter provide insight into the direction of causality by incorporating additional control variables and new statistical technologies. Voters are likely to communicate about politics, and there is a correlation between social connection and candidate/party choice. That is, since individuals select network members with similar socioeconomic and demographic characteristics and these characteristics correlate with political preferences, then individuals are effectively selecting individuals with whom they are likely to have shared candidate preferences. Only by accounting for these shared characteristics is it possible to ascertain network influence. This chapter accounts for this selection problem in two ways: first by considering the respondent's gender, race, marital status, education level, employment status, and income in the analysis and, second, by incorporating a panel study, which allows us to observe change in respondents' candidate preferences over time. By using both techniques, it is possible to overcome a great deal of the selection problem.

Data reported in this chapter address the questions of motivation: do respondents use discussant information to update their preferences and make better choices, or are they simply motivated by social pressure to appear like those around them? The sections that follow analyze each of the survey data sets individually to determine the presence of a network effect. Then the additional characteristics of the network relationships in each data set are used to explore the mechanism driving these results. It is possible to draw causal inferences from survey data without random assignment of partisan discussants. Randomly assigning discussants is unlikely to generate the type of results reported in the two preceding chapters. Network effects appear to exist mostly within those relationships where there is already a strong social tie. This generates an enormous problem for identifying network effects. Individuals choose their social networks based upon shared characteristics, a feature of networks referred to as homophily. If network effects are only present within social networks with homophily, then the sole means of identifying network effects is to control for those characteristics by which the network relationships were formed. Otherwise it is not possible to distinguish network effects from the effects of shared characteristics.

Two criteria must be met in order to demonstrate that individuals are influenced by their social networks. First, after homophily is controlled for, there must be effects on candidate choices attributable to the politics of the political network. Second, over the course of the campaign, individuals must begin to converge toward the preferences of their political networks. Both criteria are met in the empirical analyses that follow. Furthermore, it is clear that more frequent network interactions and closer social ties (particularly family ties) produce much greater effects. This suggests that these effects are likely attributable to social pressure. There are no variations attributable to the level of political information held by the survey respondents or their political affiliations.

Social Network Voting: Voting Together

Every four years American citizens cast ballots in a presidential election. Because no president can serve for more than eight years, Americans are forced to make new decisions about which candidate to choose in most presidential election cycles. The parties that win and lose elections change, and the political trends that emerge from candidate choices are fundamental to understanding American politics. Scholars believe that candidate choice is typically a function of three key elements in an individual's calculus: issue evaluations (Druckman, Jacobs, and Ostermeier 2004), image evaluations (Kinder 1978; Funk 1999), and political and social demographics including party identification, income, and education (Alvarez and Nagler 1998). There is little in this model that incorporates social network preference, yet many individuals report talking to their friends and family about politics in each election cycle. High levels of media exposure move the question of which candidate to choose into the regular public discourse, particularly in the few weeks immediately prior to the election. That discourse plays a role in an individual's choice of candidate. Individuals' social networks are particularly influential in instances where a Democrat votes Republican.

Since as far back as the Columbia School, political scientists have claimed that individuals use their social networks as resources for political information and to help determine their political preference (Berelson, Lazarsfeld, and McPhee 1954; Lazarsfeld, Berelson, and Gaudet 1948; Eulau 1963). Is it possible to explain the behavior of rogue voters, who do not appear to vote based upon their individual preferences, by focusing on their social networks? V. O. Key (1966) claimed that "switchers," individuals who vote for one party in one election and the other party in the subsequent election, constitute between 13 and 20 percent of the electorate. Are the switchers falling prey to social pressure from their political networks?[3]

How can a voter's context influence her political behavior? Voters are assumed to choose their political networks based upon their characteristics, such as their education level, marital status, income, and whether or not they have children.[4] After selecting a neighborhood network (for which this analysis will use a congressional district as a proxy) and an immediate discussion network (close friends identified by responses to the ANES), the respondent will be exposed to political discourse and behaviors from this discussion network. While many discussion partners have similar political ideologies, there is evidence that politically diverse discussion networks are common (Huckfeldt, Johnson, and Sprague 2004; Huckfeldt, Beck, et al. 1998; Huckfeldt, Levine, et al. 1998). These discussion networks have large effects on the respondent's politics. In their analysis of the 2000 ANES, Huckfeldt, Johnson, and Sprague (2004, 63) assess the influence of discussion networks on respondents' candidate thermometer scores and find "that strong partisans are not immune to the political messages that are filtered through networks of political communication." The politics of the discussion network influence each member.

How much do a discussion network's politics influence a respondent? This is a difficult question to answer, as respondents select discussion networks based upon shared characteristics, many of which correlate to political choice and expression. Thus inferences about the impact of discussion networks must account for these shared characteristics. In the sections that follow, the preferences of the individual's social network are considered the "treatment" to which each individual is exposed. Analysis focuses on ascertaining the effect of this treatment. If the mechanism that generates influence is social pressure, the individual respondent is likely to be most affected by the majority of her network, and each individual should be affected more intensely by close relationships, both in terms of geography and intensity. How well informed each voter is should have no effect on the magnitude of the discussion network treatment effect.

A Self-Identified Political Discussion Network

The Erie County study of 1940 and the Elmira Community study of 1948 report finding positive and significant effects of social networks on individual political behavior from detailed panel samples of small communities (Lazarsfeld, Berelson, and Gaudet 1948; Berelson, Lazarsfeld, and McPhee 1954).[5] In recent years, there has been a renaissance of studies of this type, conducted on different community samples to investigate the effect of social networks on vote choice, social communication, expertise, and disagreement (Huckfeldt and Sprague 1988, 1991, 1995; Huckfeldt et al. 1995; Huckfeldt 1995; Huckfeldt and Levine et al. 1998; Mondak, Mutz, and Huckfeldt 1996).[6] This literature tends to find that peer-to-peer communication affects political choices.

The applicability of community-based surveys has come into question, as many scholars claim that Americans are increasingly "bowling alone" and replacing neighborhood social interactions with online social interactions (Putnam 2000; Sunstein 2001). In February 2004 the Pew Internet and American Life Project conducted a survey on social ties in America. It found that "traditional orientation to neighborhood and village-based groups is moving towards communities that are oriented around geographically dispersed social networks" (Rainie, Horrigan, and Cornfield 2005, 2). The Pew results also indicate that respondents were likely to get advice from people online. If the Internet and other technological developments (such as nationwide long-distance cellular phone plans) change with whom voters interact, it is likely to affect their voting choices. In particular, if respondents are more likely to have discussion partners who are geographically distant, then knowledge of the respondent's geography is not sufficient to control for her political network.

This concern has resulted in the inclusion of network batteries on surveys of national probability samples, including the General Social Survey and the ANES. In particular, there is a high degree of geographic variation in the location of discussants with respect to the respondent across these surveys—for example, only 20 percent of the discussants identified in the 2006 ANES share a household with the respondent. Thus one benefit of conducting surveys to elicit the identities of individuals with whom the respondent discusses politics is that it produces data beyond that of the immediate physical geography of the respondent. Using geographic proxies may be insufficient in these cases where communication about politics can take place by phone, Internet, and other technologies, and surveys, with a set of assumptions, provide one way to understand the impact of political networks. Surveys are now being used to document and explain behaviors beyond the standard decision calculus, which considers behavior solely as a function of *individual* preference, probability of impact, or civic responsibilities. These network batteries typically ask each survey respondent to identify the names of a fixed number of individuals with whom the respondent discusses important or political matters. The names provided by the survey respondent form that individual's political discussion network.

Respondents are asked to identify a relatively small number of discussants, usually three to six, who compose their political network. These discussants are not necessarily representative of the respondent's larger social sphere but are very likely to form the respondent's primary social group. Attempts to estimate social network size suggest that the average social network contains somewhere between 290 and 750 people (McCarty et al. 2001; Killworth et al. 1990; Zheng, Salganik, and Gelman 2006). Weak social connections are not likely to be included in the small set of individuals identified by the respondent (Mutz 2006). Analysis of network surveys requires assuming that the discussants identified by the respondents are the primary influences within an individual's political network. This assumption is extremely consistent with other existing survey analysis. While a person may know several hundred people by sight or name, individuals are typically close to only a very small number of individuals. The average American, for example, has just four close contacts, and only 5 percent of Americans have eight such contacts (Christakis and Fowler 2009). These intimate contacts may also be representative of the politically weak ties to which an individual is exposed. Some political disagreement is consistently present across these self-identified political discussion networks. While this may be an underestimate of the actual amount of political disagreement individuals are exposed to through their broader network, the surveys do indicate some heterogeneity of network preferences. This heterogeneity is sufficient to identity the effects of these intimate contacts on an individual's political expressions.

Survey respondents usually are asked to provide names of individuals with whom they have discussed "government, elections, and politics."[7] They are then asked to identify a full set of characteristics of each discussant, including their socioeconomic and demographic characteristics, their relationship to the respondent, and their political preferences and choices. One concern with the analysis of these data is that the respondent will fail to correctly identify and recall all of this information.

However, Huckfeldt and Sprague (1987, 1988) and Huckfeldt, Sprague, and Levine (2000) conducted snowball surveys on political discussion partners, surveys in which an initial respondent is asked a series of questions and then asked for the contact information of her discussion partners, who are then contacted and administered the same survey. The existing snowball surveys on political discussion partners are limited, in terms of both their geographic scope and their focus on only a few specific election cycles. Yet there are remarkably consistent results with respect to the ability of respondents to describe the discussants' political preferences. Huckfeldt and Sprague (1987, 1988) found that approximately 80 percent of all respondents were able to correctly identify the political preferences of their discussants and that in the 20 percent of cases where discussants' preferences were misidentified, approximately three-quarters of respondents believed the discussant agreed with the them. In Huckfeldt and Sprague's 1996 Indianapolis–St. Louis study they also find that the respondents are 80 percent accurate when asked about the partisanship of their political discussants and that the respondents are more likely to be accurate if they agree with the discussant's true political preferences (Huckfeldt, Johnson, and Sprague 2004). This result is similar to the analysis of the Comparative National Election Project in 1992, which finds that respondents are 81 percent accurate (Huckfeldt et al. 1995).[8] The presence of misidentified politics is not a concern in the analysis of the effects of discussants on respondents, however. The respondent's perception of the discussants' preferences rather than their true preferences should drive the discussant to change political preferences. That there are more instances of misidentification that correspond with the respondent's preferences again suggests the degree to which social pressure generates conformity.

One advantage of national probability sample surveys is that they elicit independent networks, where spillovers of treatment effects are not a concern from one network to another.[9] These data have the added benefit of providing variation in the context of the respondents, so that all individuals within the network are not exposed to a common, unobserved variable. Yet these data are subject to a standard criticism of observational network data, that unaccounted environmental factors or other unobserved factors could drive the relationship between the respondent and her discussants (Shalizi and Thomas 2011; Cohen-Cole and Fletcher 2008).[10] The sole solution to this problem is to ask the necessary additional questions of the respondent to control for context, and to locate the respondent geographically and append additional data to the respondent's physical location. These questions must capture the extent to which individuals became friends because of shared characteristics (homophily) as well as their shared environmental exposures (Sinclair 2010). Thus inferences regarding the influence of discussants on respondents' political choices cannot be made without assumptions regarding the selection process, as it is possible that both respondent and discussant have identical political preferences and formed a social connection based upon those preferences.

In the research presented in both this chapter and the following, political networks were elicited by survey. Identifying such intimate discussants provides key insight into the types of influences that those who are most socially proximate to the respondent have in determining the respondent's politics. Choosing a candidate or a party identification (discussed in the next chapter) is a more private act than voting or donating. These choices are less likely to have an explicitly social, public component. Consequently, they are less likely to be affected by geographically proximate neighbors and more likely to be affected by an intimate social group. Thus the choice of a particular candidate or the decision to identify with a party is perhaps best studied via survey, where the respondent can describe the nature of the political conversations with members of the social network with whom she is most intimate.

Gore versus Bush, November 2000

The ANES data from November 2000 provide an opportunity to examine the effects on the respondent of both her immediate reported political network and her broader political network, such as her congressional district. Although neither of these are exact replicas of the respondent's true political network, they serve to incorporate a direct measurement of her network (via survey) and an indirect measurement of her network (via geography). While a voter may reside in a congressional district where she does not agree with the majority of voters, it is possible for her to have a smaller discussion network in which she is exposed to only those opinions with which she agrees. The survey also incorporates the variables necessary to ensure that the characteristics that drive a respondent to select a particular discussion network or congressional district are controlled for, and thus the consequences of exposure to differing political ideologies may be inferred. Control variables ensure that the consequences of both the larger, neighborhood-level network and the smaller, discussion-level network are visible without introducing additional correlations from selection into this network. After network selection is controlled for, contextual effects still emerge, suggesting that it is indeed possible for an individual's social network to change her political opinion.

Data from the 2000 ANES are augmented by partisan congressional district election return data.[11] The congressional district returns from 2000 are used as proxies for the partisan nature of a respondent's congressional district (Ansolabehere, Snyder, and Stewart 2000, 2001). Although congressional districts are clearly too large in some cases (in states such as Montana, for example) to serve as adequate proxies for an individual's neighborhood political experience, they are the smallest level of geographic identification available in the data set. Thus they will be used to control for the effect of the larger context within which the respondent receives political information. In the analyses that follow, however, the congressional district preferences are not distinguishable from zero. Thus, apart from their use as an example in the analysis in the 2000 ANES, they do not serve as a larger geographic proxy. The remaining analysis focuses only on the networks generated from the name-generator surveys. Each respondent was asked a series of questions about the people with whom she discusses important matters and how she believes her discussion partners voted in the 2000 election.[12] Responses to these questions define the smaller context within which the respondent receives political information. Both the discussion network and the congressional district were considered in order to determine if they affect the respondent's vote choice. There is a great deal of variance in response for the number and partisanship of discussion partners as well as vote choice; this variance allows us to estimate the contextual variable effects. Only 18 percent of respondents could name four discussants. Over 40 percent of all discussants identified were relatives of the respondents, 25 percent were coworkers, 10 percent attended the same church, and 20 percent were neighbors. The average respondent reported speaking to identified discussants a couple of times per week and believed her discussants were slightly informed about politics.

Each respondent was asked a series of questions that were used as control variables in the analysis. These questions include the respondent's marital status, income, age, race, gender, highest level of education, current employment status, length of residence in current community, whether or not the respondent has children, and whether the respondent has a good current financial situation. These variables most closely resemble the vector of characteristics on which a voter will select a neighborhood and friendship group and are thus important in balancing the data set, as they are most likely to be correlated with the particular contextual treatment. The average individual in this data set is married, has some college education, has children, is female, is in good financial status, is white, is ideologically moderate, has lived in her community for twenty-seven years, has a moderate income, and is forty-seven years old.

As noted earlier, the 2000 ANES found that many self-identified partisans voted for the opposite party. To distinguish a contextual difference across ideologies, a more nuanced measurement is needed than ideology self-reported on a seven-point scale. For this analysis, a two-dimensional latent utility score was constructed as an ideological proxy for each respondent. This variable captures more of the ideological preferences of each respondent than party identification, and it is highly correlated to party identification. This variable was constructed using the thermometer-score questions on the ANES and three supplemental variables. Each respondent was asked how they feel, where 0 is the coldest and 100 is the warmest, about a series of particular groups. The thirty-two thermometer-score questions in the ANES range from questions evaluating feminists to welfare recipients.[13] Questions about the degree of respondents' support for the president and whether they had a Democratic or Republican Party contact were also used to determine respondents' ideology.

Does a Respondent Resemble Her Network?

The 2000 ANES respondents describe their vote choice, characteristics, ideology, and partisan discussion network. Each survey respondent is

located within a congressional district, and partisan congressional returns are used as a proxy for the respondent's neighborhood context.
Clearly a congressional district is a poor proxy for a social network,
but congressional districts serve as a weak measurement for the types of
weak-tie social network influences that a respondent would experience
via neighborhood yard signs, for example. These data allow us to compare the extent to which a larger neighborhood context (based upon
congressional district returns) and a more immediate context (based
upon the partisan nature of her discussion network) influence a voter's
decision.

The 2000 ANES data demonstrate that indeed the respondents do
live in politically diverse communities; that is, there are many individuals who voted for a Democratic presidential candidate but lived in a Republican congressional district or voted for a Democratic presidential
candidate although their principle discussion network was composed of
Republicans.[14] Table 4.1 lists the percentages and raw numbers available in the data set that separate the majority political party in respondents' congressional district and discussion networks into all four possible combinations of ideology and party identification. The presence
of individuals whose vote is different from the majority party in their
network ensures that there are enough of these cases to study.

The puzzle begins when the data are tabulated by vote, by respondent ideology, and by social context. Table 4.2 shows the percentage of
instances in which a self-identified liberal voter who lived in a majority

Table 4.1. Votes by Respondents' networks' partisan majority

	Vote	
Network majority party and respondent vote	Percent	Number
Congressional district		
District Democratic, vote Democratic	29.35	344
District Republican, vote Democratic	22.28	262
District Democratic, vote Republican	24.40	287
District Republican, vote Republican	24.06	283
Total	100	1,176
Discussion network		
Network Democratic, vote Democratic	30.10	354
Network Republican, vote Democratic	22.79	268
Network Democratic, vote Republican	13.69	161
Network Republican, vote Republican	33.42	393
Total	100	1,176

Note: Data values are the percentage and number of respondents who had the indicated combination of majority-party contextual influence and presidential vote.

Table 4.2. Respondents' Presidential Votes by Ideology and Context

Respondents' presidential vote	Ideological self-placement and network majority party			
	Liberal, Dem. (percent)	Liberal, Rep. (percent)	Conservative, Dem. (percent)	Conservative, Rep. (percent)
	Congressional district network context			
Republican	.89	6.55	21.18	18.85
Democrat	12.48	15.89	18.40	5.75
	Discussant network context			
Republican	.72	7.54	11.49	27.72
Democrat	12.92	15.98	18.85	4.76

Note: Cell entries represent the percentage of respondents who had the column combination of self-reported ideology and majority-party contextual influence and row measure of presidential vote.

Republican congressional district voted for a Republican candidate or a self-identified conservative voter who lived in a majority Democratic discussion network voted for a Democratic candidate. These percentages are significantly higher than if the individual lived in, or had a network full of, individuals with similar partisanship. When these percentages are considered alone, it seems possible that voters are influenced by their context. For example, while only 1 percent of those voters who lived in majority Democratic congressional districts and self-identified as liberals voted for the Republican presidential candidate, 6.55 percent of those voters who lived in a majority Republican congressional district and self-identified as liberals voted for a Republican presidential candidate. To what extent are voters influenced by others within their congressional district? Within their immediate social circle? Are their friends embedded within their congressional district?

These results are presented for closer inspection in figure 4.1. The height of the bars indicates the percentage of individuals in each category voted for Bush. The categories are described at the bottom of each bar—the ideology of the respondent is listed first (either liberal or conservative) followed by the majority party category (Democratic or Republican). The white bar in each category denotes the congressional district effect, and the black bar denotes the discussion network effect. If there were no effect of congressional district or discussion network, we would anticipate that the height of the bars on the far left, which indicate the percentage of individuals who voted for Bush but who are self-identified as liberal and live in a majority-Democratic congressional district (white) or have a majority-Democratic discussion network (black), should be the same height as those immediately to their right, who are also self-identified as liberal but live in a majority-Republican congressional

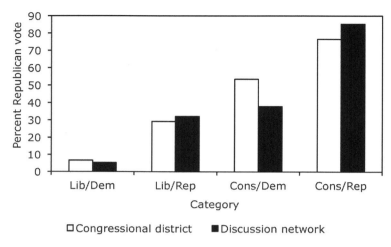

FIGURE 4.1. Self-identified partisanship combined with network or contextual effects

district or who have a majority-Republican discussion network. However, we observe a large shift in the percentage of Bush voters once
the congressional district or discussion network changes majority party.
This effect is identical for self-identified conservative respondents.[15]

All of this suggests that individuals increasingly vote like those
around them, and that the social context explanation for vote choice
is potentially appropriate, given the tabulations of the data discussed
above. One possibility is that voters are increasingly able to seek out
like-minded individuals as it becomes easier to maintain connections
across larger geographic distances. Additionally, if a voter's network is
persuasive, then it is important to understand the role of diversification
in networks for ideological stability.

The Calculus of Voting with Contextual Effects

A simple set of logit coefficients were produced to test whether both the
congressional district partisan and the discussion network breakdown
influenced voters' candidate choice. Table 4.3 presents coefficients from
both the partisan congressional district variable and the partisan discussion network variable. These covariates are included in the analysis, and
the full results can be seen in table 4.6 in the appendix.[16]

The dependent variable in the analysis in table 4.3 is an indicator
of whether or not the respondent voted for the Republican presidential candidate. Ideological distance from the Republican candidate is

established using the respondent's self-placement and placement of the Republican presidential candidate. As distance increases, the voter is less likely to vote for the Republican. Congressional district Democratic vote share and the percentage of Republicans the respondent reported in her discussion network are the key network-independent variables. These coefficients indicate that context does influence the voter's choice. As the percentage of Democrats in the voter's congressional district increases, the voter becomes less likely to vote for the Republican presidential candidate, even though this coefficient is not statistically significant. As the percentage of Republicans in the discussion network increases, the probability of voting for the Republican candidate increases. The voter's context is important.

Not only do the 2000 ANES survey respondents provide a great deal of information on their vote choice, ideology, and discussion network, they also responded to a series of questions about their own characteristics. Inclusion of these variables (such as race, age, gender, and marital status) has improved political scientists' ability to predict an individual's vote choice beyond the simple calculus of voting model (Alvarez and Nagler 1998) and should be included as control variables in any analysis.

Several of the control variables—employment status, financial status, and age—have statistically significant coefficients at traditional levels. The only contextual variable that has a statistically significant coefficient is the percent of Democrats within the respondent's discussion network, and this coefficient is positive as expected. The coefficient of the Democratic percentage in the congressional district is also positive

Table 4.3. Logit Coefficients Using Vote for Republican Presidential Candidate as Dependent Variable

Variable	Coefficient	First differences (20% to 80%)
Percent Republican discussion network	1.25	.18
	(.36)	(.05)
Percent Democratic congressional district	−.003	−.04
	(.008)	(.12)
Constant	2.72	—
	(1.49)	—
N	834	—
Pseudo R2	.72	—
Percent correctly predicted	80%	—

Note: Covariates include ideological self-placement and two-dimensional factor scores based upon thermometer score questions on marriage, education, employment status, length of residence in the community, presence of children, gender, financial status, income, race, and age. Standard errors are shown in parentheses.

but not significant. The coefficient for self-placement is negative as expected (liberal is closer to 1, conservative is closer to 7) but is also not significant. The two-factor scores are both significant, with one positive and the other negative. It is difficult to know how to interpret the directionality of these coefficients. It is possible that the factor scores are measuring both the voter's ideology and the voter's congressional district partisan breakdown.

It is difficult to draw a conclusion by simply looking at the coefficients. If only the magnitude of the coefficients is considered, the partisan breakdown of a congressional district does not seem to directly affect a voter's candidate choice, but the partisan breakdown of immediate friends does. As congressional districts are enormous entities (with populations upward of six hundred thousand), it seems likely that a voter, even once ensconced within a highly partisan district, could have a friendship network mostly composed of the opposite party. The percentage of Democrats within a respondent's discussion network positively correlates only weakly to the percentage of Democrats within a respondent's congressional district.

To clarify the consequences of the coefficients for the contextual variables, first consider the mean respondent. Her discussion network and congressional district are each approximately half Democratic. She herself self-identifies as slightly conservative, and her ideological factor scores place her in the middle of the distribution. She is likely to be married, to have some college education, to be employed, and to have lived in her community for twenty-seven years. She is likely to be female, to have children, to be in a medium financial situation, to be white, and to be approximately forty-seven years old. If she moved from a congressional district that was 20 percent Republican to one that was 80 percent Republican, it would increase the probability that she voted for the Republican presidential candidate by 4 percent. Again, however, note that these results are not statistically significant at conventional levels. Suppose that instead she were to move from a discussion network that was 20 percent Republican to a discussion network that was 80 percent Republican. This would increase the probability that she voted for the Republican presidential candidate by 18 percent.[17]

From St. George, Utah, to Santa Monica, California

What motivates a Democrat to vote for a Republican? The answer, from this analysis, appears to be an individual's social context. Were an individual to move from Santa Monica, California, to St. George, Utah—and make friends with a randomly selected group of members of the community—the probability that that individual would vote for the Republican candidate in this analysis would increase by 18 percent. The results discussed above demonstrate that, when variables influencing the choice of discussion partners are controlled for, a voter's discussion network does influence her partisan choice for president. This effect is observed when ideology and other variables that may influence a respondents' choice of congressional district or discussion partners are controlled for. A voter's social network affects her vote. This effect is robust to the inclusion of control variables: if selection is based upon these control variables, then this is evidence that this correlation is caused by influence from the other actors within the voter's social network.

While these results demonstrate that a voter's social context will influence her decision, they are unsatisfying in that the process by which this influence occurs is still not observed. The variables provided in the ANES are proxies for a voter's social network and do not provide information on the strength of social ties, for example, or whether the individuals within the network are known to each other as well as to the respondent. Also, these results make a compelling case for additional data to be collected on the partisan nature of individuals' discussion networks. It is clear that geographic proxies (such as the partisan breakdown of congressional districts) may not be sufficient, especially in this technologically advanced age. Additional survey questions will be included in the next section, which will help to address these questions.

Previous research indicated that there was correlation between the partisanship of the respondent and her discussion partners. Indeed there is a relationship between the respondent's ideology and vote choice and her contextual environment and that this relationship exists even when the respondent's choice of context is controlled for. This research has enormous implications for the causal process by which individuals may change their preferences. However, it does rely heavily upon the assumption that individuals choose their contextual networks for reasons other than partisanship. It seems unlikely that individuals choose their neighborhoods or friends because of their voting patterns, however. More likely, individuals choose their social context based on many of the other variables that have been controlled for in this analysis, some of which correlate with, but are not completely determined by, partisanship.

Obama versus McCain, November 2008

Would a registered Democrat vote for a Republican candidate? Data discussed in the preceding section suggest that an individual's social context affects her vote choice. Yet this analysis required a series of assumptions about the selection of an individual's network, including the assumption that, in isolation from a social network, an individual's ideological, socioeconomic, and demographic characteristics determine her candidate choice. Then it is possible to observe the additional social network effect on the candidate choices by comparing similar individuals with different networks. The main criticism of this assumption is that the choice of an individual's social network may be highly correlated with her candidate choice; that is, two individuals with identical social networks and characteristics will choose the same candidate, but this choice is caused by a preference for homophily and not by the influence of the network itself. This discussion in this section relaxes that assumption by observing the network preferences and the preferences of the individuals at two different points in time. Thus it is possible to observe the survey respondents converging toward the preferences of the discussants over the course of the election cycle. Furthermore, responses based upon additional survey questions make it possible to observe that sometimes a Democrat will still vote for the Democrat but be slightly more supportive of the Republican candidate if she has Republican friends.

The existing literature on this topic notes correlations between a respondent's reported discussion partner's political ideology and her own but does not provide a coherent theory describing precisely how a voter's context influences her political behavior. This section assumes, consistent with the growing literature documenting homophily (McPherson, Smith-Lovin, and Cook 2001), that voters choose their political networks based upon shared characteristics such as education level, age, race, religion, gender, and age. After selecting an immediate discussion network, the respondent is exposed to political discourse. Control variables ensure that the consequences of the discussion network on candidate preferences and choice are visible beyond those resulting from correlations based on selection into the network. After network selection is controlled for, network effects still emerge, suggesting that indeed it is possible for an individual's social network to change her political opinion. The US presidential election in November 2008 offered an opportunity to continue to investigate social network effects in candidate choice. Republican president George W. Bush could not serve another term, and thus two sitting senators, Democrat Barack Obama and Republican John McCain, competed for the seat. Because there was no current president, each voter had to make a new choice between the two candidates.

The description of the survey data used for this study that follows frames this narrative in experimental terms. If we assume that all individuals have selected into their "treatment" or "control" groups, understanding the selection into a particular network and the resulting exposure to political dialogue that follows is key to this analysis. Social network effects are then documented using several separate dependent variables regarding candidate choice and candidate preferences. A simple logit analysis indicates that the social network variables add explanatory power to the traditional calculus of voting model, which motivates the robustness tests discussed in the next section. It is then possible to conclude that, once the selection of the network is controlled for with the best methodological tools available, it is apparent that network effects do influence an individual's vote choice. Breaking down these findings by political sophistication and exposure to impersonal media then demonstrates a consistent pattern that contributes to our understanding of the mechanism by which an individual's social network can influence her political behavior and the potential implications for the presence of social network effects.

Network Panel Data

The data in this study are drawn from the 2008 CCAP, an Internet survey of registered voters that was commissioned by a group of universities and conducted by the survey house Polimetrix.[18] Respondents to this monthly panel survey were first contacted in January 2008, and in both October and postelection November 2008 these individuals were asked a series of questions regarding their political network. The discussion below uses survey questions from the January, October, and November panels to establish respondents' characteristics and preferences as well as those of their political discussion networks.

Each respondent was asked a series of questions about the people with whom she discussed politics.[19] Respondents were then asked to identify the political preferences and vote choices of the discussion partners. They were also asked a number of questions about their relationship with each discussant. These variables describe the social context within which the respondent receives political stimuli from her social network.

The number of discussion partners and their relationships with the respondent vary. Of the 1,474 respondents, 1,223 named at least one discussant.[20] More than 42 percent of all discussants were relatives, 30 percent were friends, 16 percent were coworkers, 8 percent were members of the same household, 6 percent were members of the same group, and 4 percent were neighbors.[21] The average respondent had a discussion network whose members most often lived in the same city, with whom the respondent spoke a couple of times per week on average. Respondents usually shared many characteristics with their discussants as well: 79 percent of the time they were the same race, 55 percent of the time they were the same gender, 45 percent of the time they were the same age, 44 percent of the time they had the same level of education, and 45 percent of the time were the same religion. The survey asked each respondent to identify discussants in both October and November, and many of the same individuals were identified in both months. In November, 22.24 percent of the respondents identified every name they had identified in October, and only 23.22 percent had no repeating names. The discussants were very likely to be stable components of the respondent's political life. The partisanship and preferences of the discussants serve as treatment variables, discussed in the next section, affecting the respondent's own preferences.

One of the primary advantages of this data set is its ability to control for homophily. To that end, many of the covariates described above regarding the discussion network play key roles in identifying the network effect. Additionally, this data set contains the demographic and socioeconomic profile of each respondent. Questions include the respondent's marital status, highest level of education achieved, current employment status, income, race, and gender. These questions resemble most closely the vector of characteristics on which a voter will select a neighborhood and friendship group, and thus these particular characteristics are important to include, as they are most likely to be correlated with the particular contextual treatment (McPherson, Smith-Lovin, and Cook 2001). The average individual in the survey conducted by the 2008 CCAP is similar to the average individual in the 2000 ANES, with the following characteristics: married, has some college education, is female, is employed, is white, and has a moderate income. These serve as key control variables, and data on the respondent's political preferences, media exposure, political interest, and the types of relationships with each discussant allow for a variety of tests of particular mechanisms.

Another primary contribution of this data set is that the panel nature of the data makes it possible to observe the treatment and outcome variables at different points in time. The respondent's political preferences are necessary for determining whether or not the respondent is exposed to network disagreement. To determine the respondent's ideology, a seven-point party identification variable was used, ranging from strong Democrat to strong Republican.[22] The next section describes the amount of disagreement present in an individual's political network. It is difficult to persuade a partisan to switch her vote. However, in the presence of disagreement there are shifts in the support for particular candidates, which is also explored as a potential outcome variable.

Treated with a Majority of Disagreement

The treatment variable is defined as the majority of the candidate preferences expressed by the discussion network. This is a stricter requirement than in the preceding data analysis, and if the results that emerge from this analysis demonstrate the efficacy of this network variable, this provides additional support for social pressure. That is, if the respondent identifies a majority of individuals in her network who support Obama, she is considered to have a majority-Obama treatment. In this case, the theoretical prediction is that such individuals should be particularly affected by their networks. Particularly interesting are those individuals who identified a network that is significantly different from their own partisan ideology would suggest. Each discussant's party identification and candidate choice are identified, providing several avenues to define the presence of disagreement between the social network and the respondent. I considered the average party identification of the discussion network and percentage of ballots from the discussion network to be cast for Obama. For the first, I averaged the seven-point scale for all eligible discussants. This produces an average network ideology of 3.94 with a standard deviation of 1.76, where the smallest network ideology is 1 (strong Democrat) and the largest network ideology is 7 (strong Republican). There is clear evidence of homophily in discussants' partisanship, as seen in table 4.4.

The rows of this table show the percentage of discussants whose party identification corresponds with each column label out of the total number of respondents who identified with the row label. That is, for example, of all respondents who identified as strong Democrats, 49 percent of their discussants also identified as strong Democrats, in contrast to the 6 percent of the discussants who identified as strong Democrats for those individuals who identified as strong Republicans.

One concern with using these data is that the very presence of

Table 4.4. Respondent Party Identification by Percentage Discussants' Party Identification

	Discussants (%)						
Respondent	Strong Dem.	Weak Dem.	Leaning Dem.	Ind.	Leaning Rep.	Weak Rep.	Strong Rep.
Strong Dem.	49	23	4	10	4	5	6
Weak Dem.	17	27	11	18	6	11	9
Leaning Dem.	20	17	7	40	4	7	6
Independent	8	9	5	53	4	9	12
Leaning Rep.	6	8	6	28	9	18	25
Weak Rep.	7	7	9	23	9	23	21
Strong Rep.	6	6	4	13	5	20	46

disagreement within an individual's discussion network may be endogenous to an individual's choice of discussion partners—that is, an individual may deliberately choose discussion partners with whom she agrees politically, or alternatively an individual may deliberately choose discussion partners with whom she disagrees to talk to about politics. The selection into the treatment variable then—disagreement—has the potential to cause problems in the statistical analysis and causal interpretation.

There are two arguments with respect to a respondent's choice of discussion network that suggest that the high degree of correlation between the respondent and discussion network is attributable to those characteristics that are likely to predict friendship and not political disagreement. First, some literature indicates that respondents are likely to choose discussants for shared, visible characteristics (Goeree et al. 2009), and thus we should be able to solicit the reasons for the network choice. The discussion network appears to be homophilous: 79 percent of all discussants are the same race of the respondent, for example. Second, the concern with the choice of network is with respect to the treatment variable—disagreement—and not with respect to the outcome variable (vote choice/candidate preference). It seems unlikely that individuals choose their discussion network after they have decided for whom to vote.

One potential definition of disagreement is the difference in partisan ideology between the respondent and the average discussant. Table 4.5 shows coefficients from a regression model that considers the difference on that scale between the respondent and the average discussant as a dependent variable. Independent variables include their shared characteristics in terms of race, gender, age, education level, and religion. Note that none of these coefficients are statistically different from zero, although these characteristics are typically associated with particular partisan preferences. This suggests that if individuals select their discussion networks based upon these characteristics, they do not select them based upon party identification. The second column indicates the level of homophily present in the networks based upon each of these variables. While these variables are very poor predictors of disagreement, they are very highly correlated with the respondent's characteristics. This suggests that the primary reason individuals choose their networks is homophily—being of the same race, gender, age, education, and religion (McPherson et al. 2001).

The additional questions in this survey regarding the discussion network characteristics are designed reveal the extent to which respondents have self-selected into the disagreement treatment. There is no evidence that respondents have selected their discussion network based upon disagreement; they have likely chosen their discussion network based upon shared characteristics and geography. Key to this analysis, however, is that the respondents have not selected their discussion network based upon the outcome variable, because it is upon this assumption that we are able to explore the effects of disagreement on candidate preferences and choices. The presence of network disagreement is likely to affect an individual's preferences, and as in the literature on correct voting (Sokhey and McClurg 2008; Lau and Redlawsk 1997), by determining the respondent's preferences independently of those of the discussion network, it is possible to ascertain the effect of the network on the outcome variables.

Since it appears that voters do not choose their networks for ideological similarity but instead for similarity along other covariates, it is

Table 4.5. Ordinary Least Squares Coefficients: Disagreement ($|x_{Respondent} - x_{Avg.\ Dis}|$)

Variable	Coefficient	Population homophily (%)
Percent same race	−.18 (.11)	80.78
Percent same gender	.04 (.10)	56.16
Percent same age	.06 (.10)	46.85
Percent same education level	.08 (.10)	45.43
Percent same religion	−.13 (.08)	46.68
Constant	1.41 (.11)	—
$N = 1,120$		—
Adj R2	.002	—

Note: This model is robust to the inclusion of control variables for respondent gender, race, marital status, education level, employment status, income, and an indicator if income is missing. No coefficients are statistically significant at traditional levels. This analysis includes the 1,120 individuals who defined both their own partisan ideology and the average partisan ideology of their discussion network. Standard errors are shown in parentheses.

sufficient to include these other variables as control variables in the future analyses. This will allow any remaining effect—beyond that of shared race, gender, age, education, and religion—to be attributable to political influence. The remainder of this chapter considers the treatment variable to be a binary variable indicating whether or not the majority of individuals in the respondent's network supported Obama. Networks that are evenly split will not be considered to have received positive "Obama" treatment. The treatment variable is illustrated in figure 4.2.

In figure 4.2, the height of each bar indicates the fraction of the discussants of respondents in each party identification category who fall into one of three categories—a split level of support for both Obama and McCain, more McCain support, and more Obama support. Strong Democrats have networks that are mostly supportive of Obama, for example. Fortunately, however, party identification does not completely determine each individual's network support. Respondents with mixed networks, that is, with support for both McCain and Obama, make up 22 percent of the data set (270 individuals). The presence of individuals with mixed networks or who have networks that disagree with their own party identification ensures that it is possible to identify the impact of social network effects in these data.

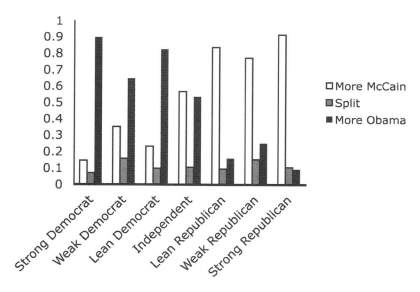

FIGURE 4.2. Discussant vote choices by respondent party identification

Measuring Vote Choice, Candidate Support, and Change

We measure three outcome variables: the respondent's vote choice, the difference between the respondent's support for Obama and her support for McCain, and the amount of change in the respondent's candidate support from January to November. In the postelection November 2008 survey, respondents were asked for whom they cast a ballot. Of the 1,101 individuals who responded that they voted for either McCain or Obama, 561 reported voting for Obama, and 540 report voting for McCain. For the second outcome variable, respondents were also asked in the postelection November 2008 survey to identify their level of support for each candidate on a five-point scale, and 1,160 individuals reported support for both McCain and Obama. We calculated the difference in their support for each of these candidates by subtracting support for McCain from support for Obama.

Our third outcome variable is the amount of change in respondents' support over the survey period. Individuals were asked about their level of support for the two candidates in January, October, and November. We observed fewer people who were neutral or who hadn't heard enough about either candidate in November than in January. To model individual-level change, we calculated the difference between the January and November reports. Approximately half of the individuals in this sample reported no change in their opinion.

The Calculus of Voting with Political Network Effects

In order to test whether discussion networks influence voters' candidate choice, a simple set of regression coefficients were produced. The results that follow support the presence of social network effects for each of the outcome variables—candidate choice, candidate support, and change in candidate support. Across all four statistical models, there is strong support for the persuasive effects of social network disagreement.

Figure 4.3 plots each coefficient for the variable that indicates whether or not the respondent has a majority of Obama voters in their discussion network across all four models. Respondents were asked to provide their race, gender, marital status, and several other characteristics likely to be correlated with their ideology and thus to affect their vote choice. The coefficients for the models with and without the control variables are presented in the appendix. The coefficients for each outcome variable are presented graphically in figure 4.3. The dots

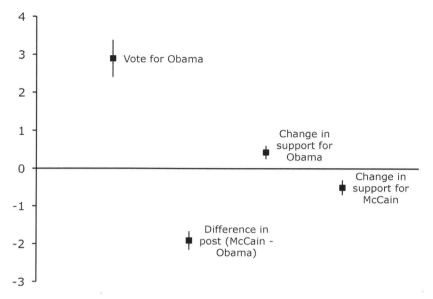

FIGURE 4.3. Estimates of social network effects
These models include control variables for respondent gender, race, marital status, education level, employment status, income, and an indicator if income is missing.

indicate the coefficient, and the vertical lines denote the 95 percent confidence interval. The dependent variable for the first model is an indicator variable that takes the value of 0 for a McCain vote and 1 for a Obama vote.[23] Indicating that having a discussion network with a majority of Obama supporters is likely to increase the probability that the respondent voted for Obama (the key independent variable), the first coefficient is positive and bounded away from zero, even after partisan ideology and other covariates are controlled for.

The second dependent variable describes the difference in postelection support between Obama and McCain. Respondents were asked to report their level of support for each of the two candidates in the postelection November 2008 panel. The difference in these responses from earlier responses to the same question is the dependent variable in the second model, where the coefficient on the effect of whether a majority of the discussion network supported Obama on that difference is represented by the second-to-the-left point estimate in this figure. Lower values indicate more Obama support, and higher values indicate more McCain support. This variable is more nuanced than the first model, which focused only on whether the respondent intended to vote for Obama. Again, the key independent variable is whether a majority of the discussion network supported Obama. Again the coefficient indicates that this social network characteristic plays a statistically significant role—a majority of discussion network support for Obama decreases the relative level of support for McCain.

The final set of estimates is based upon the change in support for both Obama and McCain from January to November. Many voters were uncertain about their preferences in January, but as the campaign proceeded, they had the opportunity to resolve their doubts. One potential mechanism for social influence is that political networks were useful in resolving this uncertainty, and determining whether this is the case is the motivation for this analysis. These are the final two coefficients. The dependent variable in this analysis subtracts the level of support for the candidate in January from the level of support for the candidate in November. Thus more negative numbers indicate a decrease in support, while more positive numbers indicate an increase in support. Having a majority of network support for Obama increases the support for Obama and decreases the support for McCain. These results specifically suggest a social network effect over the course of the campaign. Respondents provided their base level of support in January, discussant preferences were elicited in October, and then respondents provided their updated level of support in November, by which time the discussants had had an effect on the respondent. As these results demonstrate, a voter's social ties influence her vote choice.

Robustness Tests

The robustness of the results shown in figure 4.3 is demonstrated in three subsequent analyses in which the dependent variable is the vote for Obama or McCain. First, the functional form of the analysis can be relaxed and propensity score matched to determine the effect of the network. Then the sensitivity of this result can be tested via Rosenbaum bounds. Finally, the panel nature of these data can be leveraged to calculate a difference-in-differences estimate for the effect of the network. The details of each of these robustness checks are discussed below. Across all three, there is strong evidence that the network plays a key role in determining candidate choice.

Propensity score matching allows a relaxation of the linear functional form necessary to estimate the coefficients shown in figure 4.3; this method, developed by Rosenbaum and Rubin (1983, 1984) estimates a propensity score based upon the observable covariates and then matches individuals who have received the treatment to those who have not based upon their propensity score. Here the treatment variable is defined as having a majority of network members who support Obama. The propensity score is estimated using seven-point party identification, gender, race, marital status, education level, employment status, income, and an indicator of whether the income variable is missing. Matching individuals based upon the propensity score is first evaluated in terms of the similarity between the two populations, as indicated by the difference in these covariates between the groups who had a majority of network members who supported Obama and those who did not. While there are smaller differences between these populations after matching, the populations are not identical after the matching process. Results from matching without postprocessing yield a point estimate for the effect of the majority of discussants supporting Obama of .44 with a standard error of .039, clearly significant at the $\alpha = .05$ level.[24] These results indicate that the effect is robust to the linear model specification.

The second robustness test is to determine whether this finding is sensitive to possible hidden bias because of an unobserved confounder. This method of analyzing observational data was developed to assess the level of sensitivity of a particular set of results and was used to assess the causal relationship between smoking and lung cancer, for example (Rosenbaum 2002). By calculating the Rosenbaum bounds for the P values from the Wilcoxon's signed-rank test, it is possible to determine the largest possible P value that holds assuming there is no hidden bias resulting from an unobserved confounder. In this analysis, the P value would be significant at the $\alpha = .05$ level when the unobserved confounder had a coefficient no larger than 2.0. Thus this result is not very sensitive to the presence of an unobserved confounder, suggesting that the effect is robust to the presence of unobservables.

The final robustness test is to determine whether the respondents indeed became more similar to their discussants over the course of the campaign. Respondents were asked to assess their support for Obama in both January and November, and 1,038 individuals responded to both questions. The difference-in-differences estimate calculates the difference between the November and January answers for those individuals who reported having a majority-Obama discussion network and for those who did not. The difference in those differences then provides the quantity of interest. Those individuals who reported having a majority-Obama discussion network had an average difference in support from November to January of .63; they were more likely to support Obama in November. Those individuals who did not report having a majority-Obama discussion network had an average difference in Obama support from November to January of −.26; they were less likely to support Obama in November. The difference in these differences, .89, has a standard error of .07 and thus meets the standard threshold of $\alpha = .05$ and is statistically significant.

Mechanisms: Information and Social Pressure

The foregoing analysis demonstrates that respondents are clearly influenced by their discussion networks. How respondents are influenced by discussion networks may be explained by one of two primary theories.

First, networks may play a role in changing the respondent's available political information. This can happen in two channels. In one channel, networks may be key in reducing information costs (Downs 1957; Beck et al. 2002; Huckfeldt and Sprague 1995; Huckfeldt 2001, 2007; McClurg 2006a, 2006b). If this is the mechanism by which networks are effective, then individuals who experience higher costs for cognition—low-information or low-sophistication respondents—should have larger social network effects. Networks should disproportionately reduce information costs for these individuals. Survey respondents were asked to identify the positions of ten political figures; this variable serves as a proxy for the level of political sophistication of each respondent. Individuals who were unable to identify at least half of the ten positions are classified as "not correct." The remaining individuals are classified as "correct." In a second channel, networks may play key roles in exposing respondents to different information environments and thus allow respondents to deliberate regarding the quality of different arguments (Granovetter 1973; Marsden 1987; Huckfeldt et al. 1995; Mutz 2006). Again, if this is true, low-information and low-sophistication respondents should experience larger social network effects. As articulated in Mutz (2006), moderates are more likely to "hear the other side." Individuals who identified as partisan leaners or independents are classified as moderates. All others are classified as "not moderates."

Second, networks may play key roles in maintaining group membership, and the driving mechanism for network effects may be social pressure (Gerlach and Hine 1970; Bolton 1972; McAdam 1986; Briet, Klandermans, and Kroon 1987; McAdam and Paulsen 1993; McClurg 2003). Close relationships—both those that are geographically proximate and have high frequency of contact and those that are less dynamic, such as family relationships—should then have larger social network effects. Geography, frequency of contact, and family relationships are included in the survey responses.

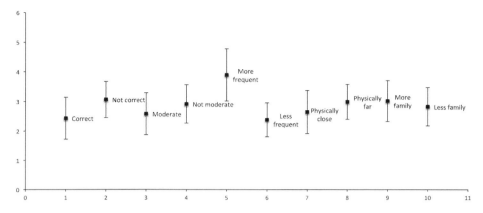

FIGURE 4.4. Coefficients on majority Obama discussant network highlighting mechanisms influencing vote for Obama

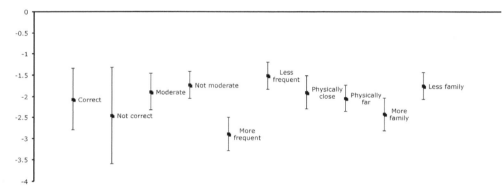

FIGURE 4.5. Coefficients on majority Obama discussant network highlighting mechanisms influencing difference in postelection support

Coefficients from a logistic regression where the dependent variable is again the choice of McCain or Obama are presented in figure 4.4. Each theory is represented with a pair of coefficients. Coefficients from a linear regression in which the dependent variable is the difference in postelection support between McCain and Obama are presented in figure 4.5.

Most of the coefficients presented here are not statistically distinguishable from each other. That is, 95 percent confidence intervals for "correct" and "not correct" coefficients overlap, for example. The same is true for "moderate" and "not moderate." The failure of these coefficients to demonstrate a trend for the correct choices or for moderates suggests that these data do not support the theory that influence is information-based. If individuals who are politically moderate and do not need additional political information do not experience larger effects, then information is unlikely to be driving the political network effect. Yet figure 4.4 shows evidence that the frequency of interaction increases the magnitude of the network effect. This is also seen in figure 4.5, where additionally family relationships also increase the magnitude of the network effect. These results are consistent with the theory that social pressure is the dominant mechanism driving these results.

A Democrat Might Vote for a Republican
If She Has Republican Friends

When ideology and variables that influence the choice of discussion partners are controlled for, it is evident that a voter's discussion network does influence her choice for president. That this effect is robust to the inclusion of control variables and model specification gives credence to the studies previously discussed in this book that have found correlation in discussion-group vote choice and ideology. This analysis advances that work by finding evidence that indeed this correlation is caused by influence from the others within the voter's social network. This previous research indicated that there was correlation between the partisanship of the respondent and her discussion partners. The results presented in this chapter indicate that there is a relationship between both the respondent's ideology and vote choice and her contextual environment and that this relationship exists even when the respondent's choice of context is controlled for. This research has enormous implications for the causal process by which individuals change their preferences. However, it does rely heavily upon the assumption that individuals choose their contextual networks for reasons other than partisanship. It seems unlikely that individuals choose their neighborhoods or friends because of their voting patterns, however. More likely, individuals choose their social context for many of the other reasons, which have been controlled for in this analysis, and that some of them are correlated with, but not completely determined by, partisanship.

By looking at the panel of data, it is possible to observe that respondents' preferences converge toward those of their discussion networks. Individuals should be talking more about politics over the course of the campaign than at any other point. Thus, at the time of the election, they should have reached as much agreement as they would reach with their network regarding candidate preferences, and this should contrast sharply with their preferences in January, when the election was not such a regular topic of conversation. These data show that convergence takes place, as respondents increasingly agree with their discussion networks.

These results demonstrate that a voter's social context will influence her decision. They provide insight into the potential mechanisms for this effect. Based upon the interactions observed, the most likely mechanism driving the presence of network effects is social pressure. Close relationships were seen to have greater effects.

Appendix

CCAP Questions

Preelection Instrument

Q: From time to time, people discuss government, elections and politics with other people. I'd like to know the names of three people you talk with about these matters. Just tell me their first names or initials.

Q: There are many ways in which people are connected to each other. Some people can be connected to you in more than one way. Please indicate all the ways that these individuals are connected to you on this list:
Rows: (NAME1, NAME2, NAME3)
Family member or relative
Coworker
Member of same household
Member of a group to which you belong
Neighbor
Friend
Professional advisor or consultant
E-contact via the Internet
Other

Q: Sometimes the people we know live close to us and sometimes they live far away. Please tell me where each of these individuals lives compared to where you live.
Rows: (NAME1, NAME2, NAME3)
In your home
In your neighborhood
In your city
In your state
In a different state
In a different country

Q: Please indicate, in general, the partisan identification of each of these individuals.
Rows: (NAME1, NAME2, NAME3)
Strong Democrat
Moderate Democrat

Weak Democrat
Independent
Weak Republican
Moderate Republican
Strong Republican

Q: Please check the candidate that you believe the following
individuals will vote for:
Rows: (NAME1, NAME2, NAME3)
Barack Obama
John McCain
Other
Will Not Vote

Q: How often do you have political conversations with each
of these individuals?
Rows: (NAME1, NAME2, NAME3)
Almost every day
At least once a week
At least once a month
At least once a year
Other

Q: In general, what do you talk about when you talk with
these individuals about politics?
Rows: (NAME1, NAME2, NAME3)
News stories about the campaign
Political issues where we agree
Political issues where we disagree
To share information
To persuade them
Other

Q: For each of the individuals below, please indicate if they
are different than you in terms of:
Rows: (NAME1, NAME2, NAME3)
Race
Gender
Approximate Age
Approximate Amount of Education
Religion

Q: Sometimes people change their opinions about politics based upon conversations with other individuals. I would like to know three people who have persuaded you to change your mind about a political issue, a political candidate, or convinced you to change a political behavior, such as turning out to vote or helping in a campaign.

Q: There are many ways in which people are connected to each other. Some people can be connected to you in more than one way. Please indicate all the ways that these individuals are connected to you on this list:
Rows: (NAME1B, NAME2B, NAME3B)
Family member or relative
Coworker
Member of same household
Member of a group to which you belong
Neighbor
Friend
Professional advisor or consultant
E-contact via the Internet
Other
Postelection Instrument

Q: Earlier we asked you for a few names of people with whom you talked about politics. Now that the election has taken place, please check the candidate that you believe the following individuals voted for:
Columns: (NAME1, NAME2, NAME3)
Barack Obama
John McCain
Other
Will Not Vote

Q: During the course of the campaign and more generally, what is the content of your conversation when you talk with these individuals about politics? Please select all that apply.
We discuss the latest news stories about the campaign and candidates.
We discuss political issues where we agree.
We discuss political issues where we disagree.

We share online links or campaign advertisements.
We try to persuade each other to change an opinion or a vote.
Something else [OPEN TEXT BOX]

Q: Please indicate which of these activities these individuals have helped you with in the course of the campaign. Please select all that apply.
Columns: (NAME1, NAME2, NAME3)
Finding my polling place
Remembering to vote
Supporting a candidate
Finding political information
Sharing political information from the Internet
Choosing a candidate
Strengthening my opinion

Q: Please identify which of these individuals know each other
Columns: (NAME1, NAME2, NAME3)
(NAME1) (NAME2) (NAME3)

Table 4.6. Original Logit Coefficients using Vote for Republican Presidential Candidate as Dependent Variable

Variable	Coefficient	Standard error
Percent Republican discussion network	1.25	(.37)
Percent Democratic congressional. district	−.003	(.008)
Factor 1	−.89	(.18)
Factor 2	4.91	(.45)
Self-placement	.003	(.13)
Married	−.22	(.46)
Education	.001	(.01)
Employed	−.25	(.34)
Length of residence	.003	(.005)
Children	−.57	(.37)
Female	−.04	(.30)
Financial status	−.31	(.17)
Income	.13	(.16)
White	−.58	(.59)
Age	−.02	(.01)
Constant	2.72	(1.49)
$N = 834$		
Pseudo R2	.72	

Table 4.7. Discussant Vote Choices: Network Choices

	0 McCain votes	1 McCain vote	2 McCain votes	3 McCain votes
0 Obama votes	102	76	78	267
1 Obama vote	79	74	104	0
2 Obama votes	95	92	0	0
3 Obama votes	256	0	0	0

Table 4.8. Coefficients across Three Models of Social Network Effects

	Coefficients			
Covariates	Vote for Obama	Difference in support	Change in Obama support	Change in McCain support
Majority network	2.89*	−1.91*	.43*	−.50*
Obama support	(.25)	(.13)	(.09)	(.10)
Party identification	−1.01*	.64*	−.17*	.14*
	(.07)	(.03)	(.02)	(.02)
Female	.38	−.12	.15	−.03
	(.25)	(.10)	(.08)	(.08)
Nonwhite	−.02	−.20	−.22*	−.14
	(.33)	(.13)	(.10)	(.11)
Married	−.67*	.36*	−.11*	.13
	(.09)	(.11)	(.09)	(.09)
Education	.05	−.15*	−.05*	−.08*
	(.25)	(.04)	(.03)	(.03)
Employed	.05	.08	−.05	.08
	(.25)	(.10)	(.08)	(.08)
Income	.15*	−.01	.01	−.01
	(.05)	(.02)	(.01)	(.02)
Missing income	1.03*	.28	.09	.05
	(.50)	(.19)	(.14)	(.16)
Religious	.87*	−.20*	−.01	−.11
	(.26)	(.10)	(.08)	(.08)
Constant	.35	−1.18*	.82*	−.00
	(.56)	(.26)	(.19)	(.21)
N	1,079	1,129	1,010	1,010
Pseudo R2	.67	.66	.19	.16

Note: Standard errors are shown in parentheses.
*$\alpha = .05$

5

Peer-Pressured Party Identification:
The Elephant in the Room

Suppose you walk into the lunchroom at a new job. Your new colleagues and associates are sitting around a big table, chatting and eating. You sit down and listen to the conversation. Your colleagues are talking about the Second Gulf War in Iraq. One after another, they all indicate that the US Army did find weapons of mass destruction in Iraq. Then, one of them turns to you and asks, "You agree that the army found weapons of mass destruction, right?" What would you say?

Most individuals agree that no weapons of mass destruction were found during the Second Gulf War. President Bush acknowledged that the intelligence that had led him to believe that there were weapons of mass destruction in Iraq was wrong. He is quoted as saying, "The biggest regret of all the presidency has to have been the intelligence failure in Iraq" (Goldenberg 2008). So you might imagine that you would tell your new colleagues and associates no, consistent with your beliefs. Since it's a new job and you don't know these people very well, though, you might imagine that you would indicate that you weren't sure. It is probably very hard for you to imagine that you would say yes when asked this question.

A significant body of research, however, has documented there is a high probability that you would say yes. This research is based upon some of the earliest experiments on the power of persuasion in small groups by Solomon Asch (1956). In these experiments, individuals came to a laboratory experiment in groups of five to seven. Unknown to the subject, however, the other four to six people were confederates of the experimenter. The entire group was shown three lines and asked to identify which line was the longest. First, each of the confederates was asked the question, and all identified the shortest line as the longest line. Then, the experimenter asked the subject to identify the longest line. Much as for the earlier question, there is a clear, correct answer. Yet more than one-third of the subjects agreed with the confederates and erroneously identified the shortest line as the longest line. Further, 75 percent of all subjects agreed at least once with the confederates when the experiment was repeated. This result is supported by extensive replication (Allen 1965; Levine 1989; Bond and Smith 1996). Why would the subjects abandon their own judgment in favor of the preferences of a small group?

It is widely believed that voters have a set of political predispositions that lead them to identify with one political party (Sears and Valentino 2007; Zaller 1992; Campbell, Gurin, and Miller 1954). It is also possible that voters update their party identification by considering each party's platform in relation to their own preferences and then align themselves with the party that best represents their interests (Downs 1957; Key 1966). In both cases, voters focus on their own personal politics, deriving from childhood or particularly salient political events. Yet, suppose voters exist as part of a small group—a political network. Voters might choose their party identification based upon their interactions with their closest friends and discussants, after which they announce a party identification that ensures the majority of their network continues to agree with them. These voters might be described as "political network" voters. The choice of party identification is driven in part by social networks, so at least some fraction of the electorate consists of "political network" voters.

In the 2008 survey described in the previous chapter, 7 of 1,026 individuals identified themselves as both liberal and strong Republicans, while 10 of 1,026 individuals identified themselves as both conservative and strong Democrats.[1] Did these individuals simply answer one of the survey questions wrong? In this data set there are also individuals who report on preferences on issues such as abortion, immigration, taxes, health care, the war in Iraq, and the environment that are different than those traditionally ascribed to the party with which they identify. This is a general trend for a small number of survey respondents whose party identification appears to be "wrong" based upon their other survey responses.

The presence of liberals who are Republican, of individuals whose latent ideology is estimated to be liberal but who identify as Republican, and individuals whose basic socioeconomic preferences and demographics suggest one party but who identify with another leads to two possible conclusions. The first is that a small number of survey respondents answer the party identification question incorrectly. The second is that an unobserved variable drives these survey respondents to their unusual answers. These individuals may not be answering the questions based simply on their own preferences but on the preferences of their social network.

The Social Foundations of Party Identification

Many people's choices are affected by their friends' and family's choices. A casual observer of human behavior would note this phenomenon among teenagers in their choice of slang, jeans, or cell phones, and recent economic field experiments have demonstrated that people's purchasing choices, vaccination choices, and retirement plan decisions are correlated with those in their social networks (Mobius, Niehaus, and Rosenblat 2005; Rao, Mobius, and Rosenblat 2006). Is there a social component that drives the adoption of a particular party identification?

Party identification is one of the most studied quantities in political science, as party identification appears to be the best predictor of an individual's vote choice (Campbell et al. 1960), but there has been little research done to clarify the process of adopting a particular party identification. Voters often appear to choose candidates based upon their partisan identification, and voters' affiliations with particular partisan identifications appear to remain fairly static (Sears and Funk 1999). Both of these empirical regularities make predicting voters' party identification an important task for political scientists. Some have argued there is a genetic component to party identification (Alford, Funk, and Hibbing 2005), while others have argued that party identification is inherited from parental influence or other childhood socialization (Jennings and Niemi 1968; Searing, Schwartz, and Lind 1973; Iyengar 1976). Fathers' party identification and other social characteristics or policy preferences have been used to predict party identification with some success (Goldbert 1966; Cassel 1983; Knoke and Hout 1974; Jennings and Niemi 1974), with the father's party identification the best predictor.

That one inherits one's party identification is a fairly unsatisfactory explanation, in particular when we think of an individual as a rational agent capable of forming political allegiances that align directly with her own preferences. It seems more likely that the individuals share a set of characteristics with their families but were the individual to form new, close ties, the strength of the father's party identification as a predictor would decrease. This is observed in the Jennings and Niemi's (1974) parent-socialization study: high school seniors have decreasing rates of agreement with their father's party identification as time goes on. Abramowitz (1983) similarly demonstrates that the partisan identification of a group of college students thrust into a liberal campus environment can be changed from the father's party identification. While it appears that political changes can trigger a shift in party identification (Fiorina 1981; Franklin and Jackson 1983; Franklin 1984), the role of the father's partisan identification continues to be positive and significant in any explanation of the adoption of party identification.

Political scientists have long been interested in party identification, not only because voters seem to be particularly attached to their party and reluctant to change, but also because party identification is a powerful predictor of vote choice (Campbell et al. 1960; Belknap and Campbell 1952; Keith et al. 1992; Miller and Shanks 1996; Stokes 1962; Converse 1966; Green, Palmquist, and Schickler 2002). In this literature, party identification is seen to be stable and often inherited. Franklin and Jackson (1983, 957) say that "party identification was seen as developing in youth, largely as a result of one's association with parents' partisan preference, and was ubiquitous in its influence over the other aspects of electoral behavior." Campbell et al. (1960) argue that party identification is an inherently social characteristic that ties individuals to particular social groups, in particular families, and which voters are unlikely to change. Achen (1992) argues that partisanship stability is still consistent with a model in which voters update their beliefs about party location. Partisanship is seen to be more stable than "beliefs about equal opportunity, limited government, and moral tolerance" (Goren 2005, 881). Green, Palmquist, and Schickler (2002, 74) report a correlation over thirteen panel surveys of .97 for individual respondent party identifications. Across the 1974 and 1976 ANES panel, Keith et al. (1986, 244) find party stability of 78 percent. Reported party stability is very high, even in data sets that do not require the respondents to recall their previous party identifications (Niemi, Katz, and Newman 1980; Jennings and Markus 1984; Green and Palmquist 1990). There is a debate, however, about whether party identification is flexible or static and, if flexible, what factors would provoke a particular switch. Were party identification completely static and predetermined, for example, and simultaneously such a good predictor of vote choice, then it seems unlikely there would ever be significant change in electoral outcomes.

Other political scientists have considered party identification to be a direct product of an individual's opinions about the current political framework (Downs 1957; Fiorina 1981; Gerber and Green 1998; Meier 1975). According to this argument, change in party identification can be explained by updates in information, so that "partisanship may undergo considerable change as events alter public confidence in each party or as changes in party leadership alter the perceptions of the parties' policy stances" (Gerber and Green 1998, 795). Many scholars have found that partisanship may indeed change (Brody and Rothenberg 1988; Franklin and Jackson 1983; Jackson 1975; Page and Jones 1979; Markus and Converse 1979; Dobson and Meeter 1974; Dobson and St. Angelo 1975; Dreyer 1973). Franklin (1984) finds that an individual's issue preferences are indeed components of partisanship, even when controlled for parental party identification, which suggests that individual partisanship is not completely inflexible.

The debate over flexible or static partisanship is central to our understanding of the very principles that guide voting behavior. If indeed individuals make candidate choices based upon partisanship, then the process of adopting partisanship is crucial in determining the relationship between individuals' political values, political preferences, and candidate choice as well as other political behaviors (Alvarez and Brehm 2002; Feldman 1988; Martinez and Gant 1990). Underlying each political behavior is an assumption about the voter's decision-making process. One component of this process relies heavily upon with what political party others in the individual's social group identify. Since Campbell et al. (1960), political scientists have known that an individual's social group is influential in her decision-making process. Campbell et al. say that partisanship change is attributable to changes such as "a marriage, a new job, or a change in neighborhood" (1960, 150). Social context has some level of influence on partisanship.

Social Identification with a Political Party

Because the salience of party identification does not change like the current choice of candidate or whether to turn out to vote, the dynamics between the party identification choices of an individual's social network and their own choices are likely to be more static. In particular, Mutz (2006) demonstrates that partisan identification is less likely to differ between individuals who are in close relationships, such as family members. Mutz documents patterns of deliberation and finds that disagreement is most sustainable in relationships described by sociologists as "weak ties"—relationships that do not require high levels of regular interaction. Thus while an individual's social network will change over time, her most constant relationships will likely drive party identification, as it is a component of conversation that is consistent across election cycles. Peer pressure in the adoption of party identification will come from close social ties.

The adoption of party identification is influenced by an individual's social network. Individuals who change their party identification do so as a consequence of political disagreement within their social group, and they are most likely to change to the party that is consistent with that of their social context. This is consistent with the literature on the stability and adoption of party identification and helps tie party identification to social group membership. Individual party identification does change, but it does so not only because of changes in the political arena but also because of social pressure.

Network effects on party identification may amplify network effects on candidate choice, as party identification is a key component of a voter's choice of candidate. Social networks are likely to play key roles in establishing a fundamental political proclivity for one party, establishing political preferences that are common across network members. Establishing the baseline for the network tie to party identification is then also key to identifying any additional effects on candidate choice; the combination of these two effects allows us to understand to what extent social networks will predict one of the basic underpinnings of participatory democracy—choice.

Political Discussants and Party Identification

Information on political discussants presented in this chapter was generated using surveys in which each respondent was asked to identify discussants with whom she has political conversations. Each individual was asked to describe her own partisanship and the partisanship of her political discussants. This allows us to examine the correlation between the two and to posit a relationship that enables the discussants to influence the partisan identification of the respondent. The survey includes a series of questions to ascertain the details of the respondent's relationship with the discussants and determine many of the respondent's characteristics. These variables were used to control for the selection of a discussant—using propensity score matching to relax the statistical assumptions necessary in analyzing these data—which then allows the discussant effect to be determined.

The first data set discussed in this section is based on an Internet survey conducted in October and November of 2006. Survey respondents provided information about political discussants that was used to examine the possibility that respondents' choice of party identification is influenced by the discussants' choices. When the respondent's characteristics and the nature of the relationship with the discussant are controlled for, there remains an effect of discussant party identification on respondent's choice of party identification.

The second data set discussed in this section uses the 2006 ANES pilot study to determine whether the discussant's partisan identification plays a role in determining the respondent's choice of party identification. Each respondent was asked twice to identify her party, once in November 2004 and again in November 2006. In the second instance each respondent was also asked to identify discussants and to describe the nature of her relationships with them. When the respondent's characteristics and the discussant relationships are controlled for, there is an increased probability that respondents will change party identification toward agreement with the discussants'. Political disagreement has a great effect on the stability of party identification and the direction of change.

Drawing causal inferences using data from an individual's social network is particularly difficult because it is possible to observe what appears to be influence from discussion partners but is actually influence from a shared environment (similar to observing a group of students who are all friends doing better in school and then realizing that they share a teacher, for example) or instead is in fact influence from a sorting procedure (similar to observing a group of students who are all friends doing better in school and then realizing that they became friends because they were all interested in reading) (Manski 1993). The problem is further complicated by the fact that it is likely that each network member exerts influence on each other. The data in this study were collected in a way that mirrors a national probability sample, and thus the individuals are unlikely to have been exposed to a common social environment. However, selection of discussants and the direction of influence are both of concern in drawing conclusions from these results.

It is difficult to draw causal inferences from observational data with potential selection biases. Thus the findings presented in this chapter rely upon several assumptions. The first assumption is that the problem of selection into a particular discussion network is controlled for by incorporating a series of characteristics about the respondent and the nature of her relationship with the discussants. These include a series of covariates about the respondent that are likely to be highly correlated with partisan discussion selection—race, age, income, educational status, political ideology, marital status, and gender—and serve as proxies for the variables that determined why each respondent selected particular discussants. Variables that describe the nature of the relationship with the discussant and the frequency of communication should also alleviate the selection problem. The second assumption addresses the direction of influence. The statistical model is set up so that the discussants will influence the respondent's choice of party identification and not vice versa. This assumption is supported by the findings of Huckfeldt and Sprague (2004), who document extremely low levels of reciprocity for discussants naming the respondent as an individual with whom they discuss political matters in their 1996 Indianapolis–St. Louis study. The nature of political discourse is such that it is likely asymmetrical with some individuals who have a particular taste for accumulating political information or particularly strong preferences for communicating political information to others. The final assumption is that the respondents are able to accurately discern the partisanship of the discussants. Studies of the ability of voters to determine this have found that there is a bias for the respondent to overreport agreement with the discussant. Huckfeldt and Sprague found in their 1996 Indianapolis–St. Louis study that respondents were 80 percent accurate when asked about the partisanship of their political discussants and were more likely to be accurate if they agreed with the discussant's true political preferences (Huckfeldt, Johnson, and Sprague 2004).

These two data sets allow us to examine the responses to identical questions asked on both an Internet and an in-person survey. Each survey asked respondents to identify discussants, and both asked respondents about their discussants' political preferences. Both surveys were in the field at the same time. However, the first data set used an Internet survey (which attempts to gather a national probability sample), while the second data set is based upon a survey that used an in-person door-to-door method. A fairly high number of respondents indicated that they had geographically dispersed discussion partners. Additionally, there is more disagreement in the in-person survey than the Internet survey. In both instances there is correlation between the respondents' preferences and those of their discussion partners. Thus the partisanship of a social network affects an individual's partisan identification.

The sections that follow provide a detailed discussion of each of the two data sets, including a summary of characteristics of the respondents to each survey. Each descriptive section is followed by an explanation of the methods used to analyze the results of social disagreement on an individual's choice of party identification, including a description of the consequences of applying a matching algorithm to select observations that are essentially identical in terms of covariates. Standard parametric procedures are applied to both the matched and unmatched data sets, and the great effect of discussant party identification supports Campbell's original hypothesis—that social ties play a role in determining partisanship. This links back into the initial theoretical framework, which argued that individuals who were socially connected would make correlated political choices. The final section explores this correlation in greater detail to better explain the underlying mechanisms. When respondents' characteristics and the nature of their relationships with discussants are controlled for, we find that each respondent's own partisanship is influenced by her discussants' party identification choices. Respondents are also seen to be most influenced by discussants with whom they have frequent conversations and who are geographically proximate.

Peer-Pressured Party Identification

The data for this study were collected as part of an Internet panel that was in the field shortly before the congressional midterm elections in November 2006.[2] Each respondent was asked a battery of questions designed to provide a standard set of covariates and then a set of questions particular to the study of social influence on politics. One advantage of this data set is that it is unlikely that the respondents were at all influenced by interviewer effects, as they were able to complete the survey in the privacy of their own homes. A disadvantage of the survey, however, is that despite the fact that their covariates were matched to a randomly drawn survey population, it is still possible that the Internet-user population is significantly different in some unobserved way than the average survey respondent. In this study in particular, it seems possible that respondents who are Internet users would have the opportunity to engage discussants who are not geographically proximate. As covariates such as income, age, and education have been matched directly to a randomly drawn survey population, this chapter assumes that the responses to the network battery are not affected despite the fact that this is an Internet population.

Each survey respondent was asked to provide up to two names of individuals with whom she discussed politics.[3] Of the 1,000 respondents, 155 were unable or unwilling to name any discussants whatsoever and were excluded from further analysis. Of the individuals who could name discussants, sixty-four were also excluded because they were either unable to identify their own party identification (twelve individuals) or were unable to identify the party identification of their discussants (fifty-three individuals). The remaining 781 individuals in the sample were able to provide both their own party identification and that of their discussion partners.

Each respondent was asked to classify her party identification on a seven-point scale ranging from strongly Democratic to strongly Republican. When asked to describe the partisanship of their discussants, respondents could choose Democratic, Republican, independent, other, or "don't know." (See table 5.1.) Table 5.2 tabulates the party identification of discussants as reported by respondents self-identified as strong, weak, or leaning Democratic or Republican or as independents. This tabulation demonstrates that respondents are more likely to have discussants who agree with their own party identification. Of the discussants of the individuals who identified as strongly Democratic, 125 (68 percent) were also classified as Democratic, whereas only 39 (18 percent) of the discussants of the individuals who identified as strongly Republican were identified as Democratic., Each respondent was assigned a binary partisan discussion treatment variable based upon her description of the partisanship of their discussants. This variable takes a value of 1 if the respondent has at least one Democratic discussion partner and is 0 otherwise.[4] Of the 781 respondents, 420 (54 percent) had at least one Democratic discussion partner, while the other 361 (46 percent) did not.

Table 5.1. Respondent Party Identification and Discussant Party Identification Raw Numbers

Respondent party identification	Discussant party identification					
	Democratic	Independent	Republican	Other	Unknown	Total
Strongly Democratic	125	29	22	4	5	185
Weakly Democratic	69	31	31	3	9	143
Leaning Democratic	87	75	35	4	10	211
Independent	34	44	25	5	14	122
Leaning Republican	32	35	59	5	12	143
Weakly Republican	34	11	72	2	5	124
Strongly Republican	39	24	145	3	7	218
Total	420	249	389	26	62	1,146

Table 5.2. Respondent Party Identification and Discussant Party Identification

Respondent party identification	Discussant party identification (%)				
	Democratic	Independent	Republican	Other	Unknown
Strongly Democratic	67.57	15.68	11.89	2.16	2.70
Weakly Democratic	48.25	21.68	21.68	2.10	6.30
Leaning Democratic	41.23	35.55	16.59	1.90	4.74
Independent	27.87	36.01	20.49	4.10	11.48
Leaning Republican	22.38	24.48	41.26	3.50	8.39
Weakly Republican	27.42	8.87	58.06	1.61	4.03
Strongly Republican	17.89	11.01	66.51	1.38	3.21

Note: Percentages indicate the portion of partisan discussants in each party reported by discussants self-identifying in each of the seven partisan categories.

The central question this chapter addresses is whether the party identification of political discussants influences the party identification of the survey respondents. Each respondent is likely to identify with a particular party based upon a number of personal characteristics, which are included in later analyses as control variables. These variables include the respondent's ideological self-placement (on a scale of 0 to 100), income, marital status, gender, age, education level, race, and homeownership. Each respondent is also likely to have established a relationship with the discussants because of a number of shared characteristics. The particular content of this survey allows for many of these characteristics to be included: the geographic distance between discussant and respondent, the frequency and method of conversation, the nature of the relationship (i.e., friend, family, etc.), and whether the discussant is likely to vote in national elections.

Each of the variables is listed in table 5.3. The average respondent is independent, has some college education, is fifty years old, and is in a fairly high income bracket. Most of the individuals in this data set are homeowners (74 percent), 63 percent are married, and 14 percent are nonwhite. Most of the respondents have discussants with whom they are geographically proximate, although 36 percent of the discussants do not live in the same city as the respondent. This statistic alone points to the need for additional survey research on the social networks of respondents, as it is clear that with 36 percent of the discussants living outside of the respondent's city, geographic proxies for social relationships are insufficient. The primary method of communication with discussants was in person (66 percent), followed by telephone (22 percent), and 56 percent of the discussants spoke with the respondent daily. More than 25 percent of discussants shared a home with the respondent, and

Table 5.3. Summary of Variables

Variable	Mean	Min.	Max.
Party identification	4.03	1	7
Democratic discussant	.54	0	1
Homeownership	.74	0	1
Female	.54	0	1
Nonwhite	.14	0	1
Education level	3.52	1	6
Marital status	.63	0	1
Age	50.79	18	106
Income bracket	8.24	1	13
Ideological self-placement	54.62	0	100
Discussant family member of respondent	.92	0	2
Discussant coworker of respondent	.36	0	2
Discussant fellow group member of respondent	.22	0	2
Discussant neighbor of respondent	.16	0	2
Discussant friend of respondent	.84	0	2
Discussant advisor of respondent	.05	0	2
Discussant Internet associate of respondent	.16	0	2
Discussant other relation to respondent	.08	0	2
Geographic distance, first discussant	1.58	0	5
Geographic distance, second discussant	2.17	0	5
Frequency of conversation, first discussant	3.51	1	4
Frequency of conversation, second discussant	3.31	1	4
Method of communication, first discussant	3.23	1	5
Method of communication, second discussant	3.01	1	5
Frequency of discussants' voting	7.6	2	8

Note: Most of these variables are categorical, and units are discerned from the survey instrument.

Table 5.4. Respondent Relationship with Discussants

Relationship	Number of discussants	Percentage
Family	734	33.01
Friend	672	30.28
Coworker	281	12.66
Group member	171	7.71
Neighbor	126	5.68
Internet contact	129	5.81
Advisor	40	1.8
Other	66	2.97
Total	2,219	100

Note: It is possible for an individual to classify a discussant into more than one relationship category, and thus the percentage column indicates the percentage of relationships that fall into each category out of all the relationships listed, not of total discussants.

the majority of relationships between discussants and respondents could be classified as family or friend, as seen in table 5.4.

This data set provides a unique opportunity to identify the effect of discussants' partisanship on respondents' because it incorporates much of the information about the relationship between the respondent and discussant while allowing for the respondent's covariates to serve as control variables in the choice of party identification.

Establishing Influence

To determine whether or not each respondent is affected by her discussants' partisanship, it is necessary to include a series of control variables along with the partisanship of the respondent and the discussant. Individual respondents will have selected their discussants because of the types of their relationships. For example, it is possible to choose to have political discussions with friends but not necessarily with family members. Furthermore, respondents will undoubtedly have selected discussants who are similar in terms of their shared socioeconomic characteristics—income, age, race, education, etc. Controlling for the respondent's characteristics and the relationship characteristics with the discussant will help to eliminate biases introduced by respondents choosing discussants with similar characteristics or having discussions within particular types of relationships. Thus all covariates described in the preceding section will be included in the analyses.

Several of the covariates have missing observations, particularly in the income category.[5] These missing values were imputed using the R package Amelia II (Honaker, King, and Blackwell 2001), and five completed data sets were produced.[6] Each of the data sets were analyzed independently, and the final statistics were computed after averaging across all five data sets.

Suppose that, as an experiment, a randomly selected group of individuals were assigned a "treatment" of either a Democratic discussant or a non-Democratic discussant. If this experiment had occurred in this data set, it would then be possible to observe the effect of the Democratic discussant treatment on party identification. However, the data set in this study is not experimental—respondents have selected their discussants, and, consequently, the treatment of Democratic discussant is not random. If we assume it would be possible to predict the type of discussant that the respondent would select based upon the respondent's characteristics and the nature of the relationship with the discussant, however, it is possible to control for discussant selection.

Because the quantity of interest here is the effect of discussant partisanship on the respondent's party identification, a subset of observations was drawn from each treatment group (Democratic discussants or non-Democratic discussants) that, in terms of their characteristics and relationships with their discussants, are practically identical. The goal is to find two individuals who both, for example, are married, have some college education, are white, have moderate income, named two family members as discussants, and are moderately liberal, but have different treatments—that is, one respondent has non-Democratic discussants and the other respondent has Democratic discussants. It is then possible to compare the effect of Democratic discussants on the respondents' party identification because the only observed variable that is different between the two respondents is the treatment variable. The process of drawing a subset of respondents from the data whose covariates are identical across the two treatments is called matching. The matching process on this data set uses all the covariates and runs on each imputed data set separately using the program MatchIt (Ho et al. 2007b). Using treatment as the dependent variable and all covariates as independent variables, a propensity score is estimated for each observation using a logistic model. Based upon that propensity score, a genetic-matching algorithm is used to determine the optimal number of observations to be included in each matched data set (Diamond and Sekhon 2007).[7]

To determine the average treatment effect of being exposed to Democratic discussants, the matched data were combined into a single data set and fit using both a linear model and an ordered logit.[8] The linear model does not capture the categorical nature of the respondent's party identification as the ordered logit will. Party identification is fit to a seven-point-scale (with 1 being strong Democrat and 7 being strong Republican), and the advantage of the linear model is to permit the incorporation of all the data into a single estimate of the mean effect of a Democratic discussant. Ordered logit is more appropriate, as the respondent's party identification is not a continuous variable. The seven-point party identification variable was used instead of the three-point party identification variable not only because more respondents were able to categorize themselves using the seven-point variable, but also because it allows for greater precision in understanding an individual voter's party identification choice. Analysis computed using a three-point party identification (Democratic, Republican, or independent), however, produces similar results.

The Effect of a Democratic Discussant

The effect of having a Democratic discussant is presented in table 5.5. Here the dependent variable is the seven-point party identification measurement, and the quantity of interest is the coefficient on the partisan discussant treatment variable.[9] The covariates were included as controls in the analysis. In the linear model, the first differences are presented using the covariates at their means and comparing the expected value of having a Democratic discussant with the expected value of having a non-Democratic discussant. This produces an effect of almost 1 point on the seven-point party identification scale and is statistically significant at traditional values. The difference in probabilities from the ordered logit supports this finding as well. Here the probability of falling into a particular partisan category is computed conditional upon having Democratic discussants or not while holding all covariates at their means. If there is an effect of discussants, then the pattern of probabilities should appear as it does in table 5.5, with the differences in probabilities for the Democratic identification positive and the Republican identification negative. If there is a discussant effect, then the probability of being a Democrat conditional upon having Democratic discussants should go up, while the probability of being a Democrat conditional upon having non-Democratic discussants should go down. Thus the difference between these two should be positive. Similarly, if there is a discussant effect, then the probability of being a strong Republican conditional upon having Democratic discussants should go down, while the probability of being a strong Republican conditional upon having non-Democratic discussants should go up. The difference between these two should be negative. Interestingly, the magnitude of the differences also changes appropriately throughout the table.

The interpretation of these results as causal relies upon a series of assumptions discussed in the introduction to this chapter. The results appear to be of such high magnitude that they are likely partially attributable to selection based upon shared, unobserved variables. It is possible

Table 5.5. Treatment Effects

	Mean	Std. dev.
Ordinary least squares quantity		
E [Party | Dem. discuss.] − E [Party | No Dem. discuss.]	−.9172	.1471
Ordered logit quantity		
P (Strong Dem. | Dem. discuss.) − P (Strong Dem. | No Dem. discuss.)	.122	.092
P (Weak Dem. | Dem. discuss.) − P (Weak Dem | No Dem. discuss.)	.038	.056
P (Lean Dem. | Dem discuss.) − P (Lean Dem | No Dem. discuss.)	.016	.089
P (Indep. | Dem. discuss.) − P (Indep. | No Dem. discuss.)	−.012	.05
P (Lean Rep. | Dem. discuss.) − P (Lean Rep | No Dem discuss.)	−.026	.053
P (Weak Rep. | Dem. discuss.) − P (Weak Rep | No Dem. discuss.)	−.037	.048
P (Strong Rep. | Dem. discuss.) − P (Strong Rep. | No Dem. discuss.)	−.1	.09
N = 2,968		

Note: These estimates are calculated after pooling all five imputed and matched data sets. Only the coefficient calculated with OLS is statistically significant at traditional levels.

that part of the selection problem has not been solved by inclusion of covariates or that respondents have overreported their discussants' partisanship in line with their own. Fortunately, there is a sufficiently large effect of discussant party identification that at least at the rate of overreporting that is measured in the existing literature, overreporting of similar partisanship is unlikely to encompass the entire observed effect (Huckfeldt, Johnson, and Sprague 2004). There does appear to be an effect of discussant party identification on respondents' choice. This effect is the marginal effect of discussant party identification alone, as many of the respondents' covariates are included in the analysis, including variables that describe the nature of the respondent's relationship with the discussant.

Mechanisms for Social Influence

The presence of a social network effect in party identification indicates that individuals are influenced by their social networks, and this effect is consistent with the existing literature on the parent-child socialization of party identification. Additionally, the inclusion of the other covariates on the survey offers insight into the mechanism driving this result.

To document disagreement in terms of partisan identification and gain a better understanding of what sorts of relationships sustain it, a variable was created that calculates the average of the discussant party identifications in a three-point party identification scale. This variable ranges from 1 to 3, with an average of 1.98. A variable to document the amount of disagreement in the relationship was then calculated by determining the distance between the respondent's three-point party identification and that of the average discussant. This variable ranges from 0 to 2 and has an average of .45.

It is then possible to simply look at the correlations between the disagreement variable and several of the other variables in the data set. These correlations provide insight into the mechanisms that drive the empirical results. The indicator variable for family, the variable to describe close geographic proximity, and the variable to describe high frequencies of interaction are all associated with close personal relationships—instances in which there would likely be more agreement, evidenced by the effectiveness of social pressure. High frequency of interaction and family relationships are both weakly correlated with lower levels of disagreement. Correlation between disagreement and the average geographic distance between discussants and respondent demonstrates that these variables are very slightly positively correlated.

There is more disagreement in relationships that have a greater geographic distance. There is also less disagreement when the primary medium for communication between the respondent and the discussants is in-person conversation.

These correlations have implications for the interpretation of the results. If the discussants' partisan identifications have real effects on the respondent's choices, then one reasonable interpretation might be that the closer the relationship between the respondent and the discussant for social interactions, the more likely the agreement in party identification. This evidence also supports the theory that the mechanism that drives these results is social pressure.

Correlation between the respondent's level of education or income and amount of disagreement is barely positive—individuals who have greater constraints for information should be more willing to seek out information from their social networks if there is an information or deliberation mechanism at work driving this result.

Dynamic Party Identification: A Social Network Explanation

This data set uses the 2006 ANES pilot study to determine whether the discussant's partisan identification plays a role in determining the respondent's choice of party identification. Each respondent was asked twice to identify her party, once in November 2004 and again in November 2006. In the second instance each respondent was also asked to identify a group of political discussants and to describe the nature of those relationships. When respondents' characteristics and discussant relationships are controlled for, there is an increased probability that each respondent will change party identification toward agreement with the discussants' party identification. These findings have implications for the study of party identification, particularly regarding adoption of new party identifications.

These data were generated by face-to-face interviews as part of the ANES pilot study in fall 2006. A total of 665 individuals were interviewed, each of whom had been interviewed in the fall of 2004. Each respondent was asked a series of questions to identify her own personal characteristics during the 2004 survey. During the pilot survey in 2006, each respondent was asked to describe some of the characteristics of their discussion networks and to provide additional details about the relationship with each discussant. These data are of particular use for two reasons. First, they provide a rare opportunity to glean insight into the characteristics of respondent-discussant relationships. Further knowledge of the respondent's discussion network is key to understanding how the discussants might influence the respondent's political behavior, and these variables were used as control variables to determine general discussant effects.

Second, the split timing of this survey provides insight into change in party identification. Each respondent was asked for her party identification in both the 2004 and 2006 survey instruments. Thus it is possible to produce an indicator variable set at 1 if the respondent's answer changed from 2004 to 2006 and 0 otherwise. Of the 661 respondents who answered both party identification questions, 198 reported a different party identification in 2006 than in 2004. The first component of the analysis identifies the factors that may influence a respondent's change in party identification. Table 5.6 shows the party identification switch for those individuals who changed party from 2004 to 2006. Most of the individuals who switched parties initially indicated that they were independent in 2004. One of these individuals reported Democratic Party identification in 2006, twenty-eight reported Republican Party identification in 2006, ten reported no preference in party identification in 2006, and eight reported having other party identification in 2006.

Each of the variables included in the analysis is incorporated in table 5.7. The table is broken down into two categories: the characteristics of the respondent and the average characteristics of the discussion network. Each respondent names approximately two discussants, and almost a third of the respondents report a different party identification. The average respondent is female, in a middle income bracket, is almost fifty years old, is married, has some college education, is employed, is white, and is a homeowner. Only 20 percent of the respondents report being parents. The average respondent is ideologically located in the middle of a 0 to 10 scale and has some interest in politics.

On average respondents perceive discussants to have more interest

Table 5.6. Respondent Party Change, November 2004 to November 2006

	Democrat 2006	Independent 2006	Republican 2006	No pref. 2006	Other 2006
Democrat 2004	—	13	4	2	2
Independent 2004	61	—	28	10	8
Republican 2004	18	23	—	0	5
No preference 2004	9	5	4	—	1
Other 2004	2	0	0	0	—

Note: The values in this table indicate the number of individuals who reported changing their party identification from the row category (their 2004 response) to the column category (their 2006 response).

Table 5.7. Summary of Variables

Variable	Mean	Min.	Max.	N
Respondent characteristics				
Party change	.3	0	1	661
Total discussants	1.86	0	3	661
Fraction network disagreement in 2004	.35	0	1	661
Fraction network disagreement in 2006	.30	0	1	661
Female	.54	0	1	661
Parent	.21	0	1	661
Income bracket	12.07	1	23	661
Age	49.75	18	90	661
Marital status	.56	0	1	661
Education level	14.2	4	17	661
Employment status	.67	0	1	661
Nonwhite	.18	0	1	661
Homeowner	.78	0	1	661
Ideological self-placement	5.12	0	10	632
Interest in politics	2.21	0	5	661
Discussant characteristics				
Interest in politics	2.41	0	5	468
Perception of disagreement	3.62	1	5	467
Intensity of relationship	1.94	1	5	468
Frequency of conversation	49.67	0	182	314
Identity as strong partisan	.66	0	1	439
Geographic distance (in minutes)	320.28	0	18,000	416
Network density	1.02	0	3	661

in politics, and the average discussion network is reported to have a moderate amount of disagreement and a low level of relationship intensity. The average discussion network communicates with the respondent fifty days a year and has many strong partisans. Interestingly, the average discussant is reported to be 320 minutes away from the respondent. (This fact alone has implications for using geographic statistics as proxies for network measurements.) Approximately one pair of the discussants communicates regularly with each other.

Two other variables were produced to evaluate the amount of disagreement to which the respondent has been exposed. This disagreement variable was calculated by dividing the total number of discussants whose partisanship disagreed with the respondent's in November 2004 by the total number of discussants provided by the respondent. Thus as the respondent's political discussion network becomes more homogeneous, the disagreement variable decreases. Each of the variables was calculated using the respondent's party identification in November 2004 and November 2006, and subsequent discussion of these variables refers to them in terms of percentage of disagreement in 2004 and 2006. The percentage of disagreement within each network is documented in

Table 5.8. Discussion Network Disagreement, November 2004 and November 2006

Network disagreement	November 2004	November 2006
None disagree	325	343
One in three disagree	92	112
One in two disagree	29	30
Two of three disagree	95	89
All disagree	120	87
N	661	661

Note: Respondents could name up to three discussants; thus the proportion of disagreement with discussants may be none (0%), one- or two-thirds (33 or 67%), half (50%), or total (100%).

table 5.8. Note that there is significantly more reported disagreement in party identification in 2004 than there is in 2006.

It is assumed here that voters are able to accurately determine the partisanship of their social connections. Studies of the ability of voters to determine this have found that there is a bias for the respondent to overreport agreement with the discussant. Huckfeldt and Sprague found in their 1996 Indianapolis–St. Louis study that the respondents were 80 percent accurate when asked about the partisanship of their political discussants and that respondents were more likely to be accurate if they agreed with the discussant's true political preferences (Huckfeldt, Johnson, and Sprague 2004). Individual's discussion networks may have changed during this time span, so the characteristics of the discussants whom they identify in 2006 may be different from those of their principal discussants in 2004, which complicates the identification of the causal mechanism. However, this data set provides a rare opportunity to observe individual partisan reports and responses regarding discussant characteristics.

Partisanship at Two Points in Time

The advantage of this particular survey is that it allows simultaneous observation of the partisanship of the respondent and her discussion network at two distinct points in time. This allows us to test two hypotheses about change in party identification.

The first hypothesis is that if the party identification of the respondent in November 2004 is different from the party identification of her discussants, the probability that the respondent has changed party identification in November 2006 will increase. It is possible to test this hypothesis by documenting whether or not the respondent has changed her party identification and then using the percentage who disagreed with discussants in 2004 as an explanatory variable. If the impact of disagreement in 2004 is positive, controlled for the selection of the discussants, then indeed the increased level of disagreement is a good predictor that the individual respondent will change party identification. To evaluate this hypothesis the statistical model will use an indicator for whether or not the individual has changed parties as a function of percentage who disagreed in 2004, the respondent's characteristics, and the discussant characteristics.

The second hypothesis is that if the party identification of the respondent in November 2004, controlled for the change in party identification, is different than the party identification of the discussants, controlled for the selection of the discussants and whether the respondent has changed parties, the probability that the respondent disagrees with the discussants in November 2006 will decrease. That is, if the respondent switches parties, it will be toward the direction of the discussants' party identification. To evaluate this hypothesis the statistical model will describe percentage who disagreed in 2006 as a function of whether the individual has changed parties, percentage who disagreed in 2004, the respondent's characteristics, and the discussant characteristics.

Both hypotheses were tested in three separate analyses. The first model includes only the variables that are the focus of this analysis. The second model incorporates the respondent characteristics as control variables; these include ideological self-placement, homeownership, race, employment status, education level, marital status, age, income, gender, and whether the respondent is a parent. The third model adds a layer incorporating not only the respondent-specific covariates but also those of the discussion network; these include the respondent's interest in discussing politics, the closeness of the relationship with the discussants, the frequency of conversation with the discussants, the geographic proximity of the discussants, and the discussant network density. Given the small number of observations, one disadvantage of incorporating the discussant characteristics is missing data, which further decreases the number of observations available for analysis. Fortunately, however, all models produce similar results.

Dynamic Influence

Coefficients on the variables that are the focus of this analysis from each statistical model are presented in table 5.9 and table 5.10. Note here that all quantities of interest are statistically significant at traditional levels and have signs that support both hypotheses. Table 5.9 presents

Table 5.9. Logit Coefficients and Effect of Disagreement in 2004 on Change in 2006

	Coefficient	Controls	N
Percent disagreement 2004	1.28* (.22)	—	661
Percent disagreement 2004	1.49* (.25)	Respondent characteristics	584
Percent disagreement 2004	3.39* (.58)	Respondent and network characteristics	265

Note: The dependent variable is an indicator of whether or not the respondent had changed partisan affiliations between 2004 and 2006. The independent variable of interest is the percentage of a respondent's discussion network that had a different partisan label than she did in 2004. Three separate models are presented here: one considering only the percentage of disagreement; one considering percentage of disagreement and respondent characteristics; and one considering percentage of disagreement, respondent characteristics, and network characteristics. Standard errors are shown in parentheses.
* $\alpha = .05$.

Table 5.10. Ordered Logit Coefficients and Effect of Change on Disagreement in 2006

Variable	Coefficient	Controls	N
Change	−1.76* (.26)	—	661
Percent disagreement 2004	6.85* (.37)		
Change	−1.63* (.27)		
Percent disagreement 2004	6.97* (.40)	Respondent characteristics	584
Change	−1.48* (.37)		
Percent disagreement 2004	7.25* (.62)	Respondent and network characteristics	265

Note: The dependent variable is the fraction of disagreement within a respondent's discussion network in 2006. The independent variables of interest are an indicator for whether or not the respondent had changed partisan affiliations between 2004 and 2006 as well as a measurement of the partisan disagreement within a respondent's discussion network in 2004. Three models are considered: one considering simply the variables of interest; one that adds the respondent characteristics; and a third that includes both respondent and network characteristics. Standard errors are shown in parentheses.
*$\alpha = .05$.

each of the coefficients on the variable of percentage of disagreement in 2004. Each of these coefficients is positive, which can be interpreted as meaning that as disagreement between the respondent's party identification and the discussants' party identification increases, the respondent is increasingly likely to report a different party identification in November 2006. Table 5.10 presents each of the coefficients on both the percentage of disagreement in 2004 and the partisan change indicator. Respondents who had disagreement in their discussion network in 2004 are likely to have disagreement in their discussion network in 2006. When disagreement in the discussion network in 2004 is controlled for, however, as the probability that the respondent changes party identifications increases, the amount of disagreement in the discussion network in 2006 will decrease. That is, as change increases, the amount of disagreement in 2006 decreases.

Again, there is evidence of social pressure. Increasing geographic distance correlates with increased disagreement between the respondent and the discussants, and increasing the frequency of conversation decreases the disagreement. There are also small correlations between employment status, education level, and income with increased disagreement. Yet the correlation with the respondent's interest in politics is almost zero. These correlations accord with a theory of social pressure.

Flexible Party Identification

The number of individuals who are clearly liberal and self-identify as Republican or who are clearly conservative and self-identify as Democratic is fairly small. Yet their presence in survey data suggests some flexibility with respect to party identification.

The results here demonstrate the social pressure component in the adoption of party identification. The existing literature has drawn the conclusion that there are influences from within families (either genetic or parental influence). This chapter demonstrates that party identification is influenced by the respondent's social connections; thus the parental studies may now be extended to larger social units of influence. The magnitude of the results here is quite large and suggests that social influence plays an enormous role in the respondent's choice of party identification.

These findings relate directly to the literature on political disagreement within social networks. Mutz (2006) and Huckfeldt, Johnson, and Sprague (2004) have documented correlations in party identification and candidate choice within voter's social networks. Mutz (2006) suggests that voters should be encouraged to sustain more "weak ties," as those are the relationships within which political disagreement can occur. The findings in this chapter support the conclusion that there will be more disagreement within relationships that have less frequent conversation and more geographic distance and suggest that the frequency of those conversations plays a role in party identification.

This in turn suggests that a social pressure component of party identification could derive from a rational-choice framework. Voters do appear to exhibit other rational behavior, such as voting strategically (Alvarez and Nagler 2000). Suppose that voters simply want to behave like those around them because they find political disagreement distasteful. Voters update their information about which party is most supported by their network from communication within their social network. If this is the case, then the combination of finding influence from discussants and of finding that more frequent discussants have greater influence gives additional credence to this possibility. Correlation in party identification, controlled for the respondent's characteristics and the nature of the discussant relationship, improves understanding of the role of social groups in determining an individual's political choices. A voter's discussion network plays an enormous role in determining her choice of party identification. The partisanship of an individual's discussion network appears to affect not only the probability that the individual will change party identification but also the party to which the individual will change.

An alternative explanation is that the respondents are all influenced by policy changes in the time between surveys in 2004 and 2006. Given the outcome of the congressional midterms and the electorate's overall disapproval of the war in Iraq, as well as the fact that there are more voters who switch to Democratic or independent party identifications than who switch to Republican, it seems possible that the voters in this study are all simultaneously influenced by a change in party location. However, the analysis attempts to incorporate this possibility by controlling for the respondent's ideological self-placement, so that a change in party identification may not be entirely explained by political events.

Throughout the literature, regardless of whether party identification is seen as stable or flexible, party identification is clearly a powerful predictor of vote choice. This analysis demonstrates that party identification is a component not only of transitive presidential approval but of social group membership. Individuals identify with political parties in much the same fashion that they identify with other social identifying characteristics, and thus political identification shifts occur only when the individual has begun to reexamine her own group memberships. These findings have important implications for understanding polarization in America and the role of heterogeneous political networks in providing moderate political preferences. Party identification, say Campbell et al. (1960, 133), "raises a perceptual screen through which the individual tends to see what is favorable to his partisan orientation. The stronger the bond, the more exaggerated the process of selection and perceptual distortion will be." If individuals are influenced by their social networks to choose party identifications similar to those around them, and if party identification biases an individual's opinions in any particular direction, then it becomes increasingly necessary to encourage debate and friendship across parties to maintain a politically balanced electorate.

Appendix

November 2006 Survey Questions

1. From time to time, people discuss government, elections and politics with other people. I'd like to know two people you talk with about these matters. These people might or might not be relatives. Just tell me their first names or initials.[10]

2. There are many ways in which people are connected to each other. Some people can be connected to you in more than one way. For these relationships, please indicate all the ways (NAME1) is connected to you on this list:
   Family member
   Coworker
   Member of a group to which you belong
   Neighbor
   Friend
   Professional advisor or consultant
   E-contact via the Internet
   Other

3. There are many ways in which people are connected to each other. Some people can be connected to you in more than one way. For these relationships, please indicate all the ways (NAME2) is connected to you on this list:
   Family member
   Coworker
   Member of a group to which you belong
   Neighbor
   Friend
   Professional advisor or consultant
   E-contact via the Internet
   Other

4. Sometimes the people we know live close to us and sometimes they live far away. Please tell me where (NAME1) lives compared to where you live.
   In your home
   In your neighborhood

In your city
In your state
In a different state
In a different country

5. Sometimes the people we know live close to us and sometimes they live far away. Please tell me where (NAME2) lives compared to where you live.
In your home
In your neighborhood
In your city
In your state
In a different state
In a different country

6. There are many ways to communicate with people. Most of the time, what is the predominant way in which you communicate with (NAME1):
Phone
Email
In person
By instant message
By mail

7. There are many ways to communicate with people. Most of the time, what is the predominant way in which you communicate with (NAME2):
Phone
Email
In person
By instant message
By mail

8. Thinking about how often you usually talk to (NAME1), on average, do you talk to (him/her):
Almost every day
At least once a week
At least once a month
Less than once a month

9. Thinking about how often you usually talk to (NAME2), on average, do you talk to (him/her):
Almost every day
At least once a week
At least once a month
Less than once a month

10. In general, would you say (NAME1) is a:
Democrat
Republican
Independent
Something else.

11. In general, would you say (NAME2) is a:
Democrat
Republican
Independent
Something else

12. As far as you know, would you say that (NAME1) is a:
Strong (Democrat/Republican/Independent)
Moderate (Democrat/Republican/Independent)
Weak (Democrat/Republican/Independent)

13. As far as you know, would you say that (NAME2) is a:
Strong (Democrat/Republican/Independent)
Moderate (Democrat/Republican/Independent)
Weak (Democrat/Republican/Independent)

14. As far as you know, does (NAME1) vote in national elections:
Almost always
Sometimes
Almost never
Never

15. As far as you know, does (NAME2) vote in national elections
Almost always
Sometimes
Almost never
Never

2006 ANES Pilot Study Questions

Q: During the last six months, did you talk with anyone face-to-face, on the phone, by email, or in any other way about [things that were important to you/government and elections], or did you not do this with anyone during the last six months?
Yes, did talk
No, did not talk
Don't know
Refused

Q: What are the initials of the people who you talked with face-to-face, on the phone, by email, or in any other way during the past six months, about [things that were important to you/government and elections]?

Q: For each name, what is that person's gender?
Male
Female

Q: How close do you feel to [NAME 1/NAME 2/NAME 3]?
Extremely close
Very close
Moderately close
Slightly close
Not close at all

Q: During the last six months, about how many days did you talk to [NAME 1/NAME 2/NAME 3]?

Q: First think about [NAME 1] and [NAME 2]. During the last six months, about how many days would you guess they talked to each other?

Q: Now think about [NAME 1] and [NAME 3]. During the last six months, about how many days would you guess they talked to each other?

Q: Now think about [NAME 2] and [NAME 3]. During the last six months, about how many days would you guess they talked to each other?

Q: In general, how different are [NAME 1 / NAME 2 / NAME 3]'s
   opinions about government and elections from your own
   views?
   Extremely different
   Very different
   Moderately different
   Slightly different
   Not different at all

Q: Generally speaking, does [NAME 1 / NAME 2 / NAME 3]
   probably think of [himself/herself] as a Democrat, Republi-
   can, Independent, or what?
   Democrat
   Republican
   Independent
   Other
   No preference

Q: Would [he/she] call [himself/herself] a strong [Democrat/
   Republican] or a not very strong [Democrat/Republican]?
   Strong
   Not very strong
   Don't know
   Refused

Q: Does [he/she] think of [himself/herself] as closer to the
   Democratic Party or the Republican Party?
   Closer to Democratic
   Closer to Republican
   Neither

Q: How interested is [NAME 1 / NAME 2 / NAME 3] in
   information about what's going on in government and
   politics?
   Extremely interested
   Very interested
   Moderately interested
   Slightly interested
   Not interested at all

Q: How much time would it take to drive from your home to
[NAME 1 / NAME 2 / NAME 3]'s home?
Time given
Can't drive there
Lives with [NAME]

6 Conclusion: Social Pressure and the Democratic Experiment

Suppose there are a few extreme citizens who always vote. The bulk of other citizens are political moderates, but they vote much less often. They shirk from voting because of the time and effort needed to cast a vote as well as the informational challenge of identifying the "right" candidate. This results in elected officials whose policies deviate substantially from interests or preferences of the bulk of the populace. Suppose, though, that one day a neighbor comes to the door and asks the shirker to turn out to vote as a personal favor. Would the shirker be able to say no?

This book argues that in many circumstances the shirker would succumb to the influence of the neighbor. The shirker would vote. Individuals are highly susceptible to social pressure from their political networks: the family, friends, and neighbors with whom they have political conversations. As individuals, they do not want to pay the costs to participate. They would prefer to shirk. Their participation is sustained, however, by adherence to social norms upheld by their social networks. These social norms are critical for democracy. The loss of the individual willingness to participate generates a huge loss for society such as in the example above: if none of the moderates cast ballots, they will be represented by extremists.

Social pressure is good for political participation but raises the question of why each individual citizen votes.

Social pressure influences citizens in positive and negative ways, and the resulting normative implications are twofold. On the one hand, democratic theorists may be negatively predisposed to the concept of a social citizen, an individual who succumbs to the preferences of her social network. In the ideal democracy individuals' preferences are treated equally, but in reality inequities in participation and responsiveness exist (Bartels 2008; Gilens 2005). The nature of social networks accentuates another source of inequality—that is, the extent to which one shapes the behavior of others. Individuals lose some of their individual autonomy and base their political decisions on the preferences of others. When it comes to making decisions about voting or identifying with a party, social networks—which often come together based on factors unrelated to political interests—may shape those preferences. In this case, expressed behaviors will reflect not only individuals' political interest but also the interests of those around them, and these interests may not cohere. On the other hand, the pressures from the social network sustain a participatory democracy in which civic duties are maintained as part of the social norm. Social pressure can promote participation and activity among those who otherwise would not act. Normative theorists must grapple with the double-edged nature of these consequences as they develop theories that recognize the role of groups. This becomes particularly relevant as the nature of social networks evolves with changing media technologies. Social media platforms provide an opportunity to give voice to those citizens for whom the cost of participating was prohibitive by reducing the amount of time needed to organize, making information more readily available, and allowing social contacts to pool political resources. Yet these platforms also make each individual citizen more vulnerable to social pressure about politics.

Political scientists have described protests, such as those that took place during the civil rights movement, as sustained or generated by social networks (Chong 1991; McAdam and Paulsen 1993). This kind of political mobilization involves the most public acts of civic participation, and instances of large-scale public protests are quite rare. Yet the social life that generates high levels of participation in social movements is constant. This book focuses on smaller acts of political participation—casting a ballot, donating to a campaign, choosing a candidate, and identifying with a party—and demonstrates that these kinds of political participation are also sustained by social networks. Individuals do not confront the myriad of political choices in a participatory democracy in isolation. Political choices—party identification and which candidate to vote for—are affected by those of one's social network. Participation decisions—the decision to cast a ballot, the decision to donate to a campaign—are based upon the norms and behavior of the social network. To this extent, then, an individual is part of a social framework in which she does not operate independently. She is not an atomistic actor who makes political decisions in isolation. Political social networks play large roles in democratic outcomes: across participation and choice decisions there is a role for the social citizen. The social citizen is a public citizen located in a social network, whose voiced social political norms of sincere civic expression lead to collective civic action. Models that seek to explain political attitudes and behaviors need to account for social networks. This is a significant departure from most approaches, which assume that the locus of citizens' actions lies entirely within the individual, as an independent actor. Not only do social surroundings provide information for individuals' calculi, but social networks and their nature in fact determine the extent of each citizen's democratic participation.

Empirical Patterns of Network Influence

This book has demonstrated four ways in which a social citizen has influence over others. In settings as diverse as South Los Angeles and the Chicago suburbs, there is empirical evidence of network influence. The role of the social citizen is defined in four political behaviors: casting a ballot, donating to a campaign, choosing a candidate, and announcing a party identification. For all of these behaviors, there is empirical evidence of network influence.

First, the social citizen influences others to cast a ballot in an election. The results of two randomized field experiments demonstrate that if the social citizen has internalized a social norm of behavior, her network will observe (and potentially learn) this norm. Social citizens who subscribe to the social norm of voting can increase the number of ballots that are cast by individuals in their community. Neighbors are more efficacious than strangers. Individuals who live with others who have internalized the social norm of voting are more likely to participate if they receive a mobilization postcard than individuals who live with others who have not internalized the social political norm. In this instance, networks are observed geographically. Neighbors and strangers are not defined by explicit social ties but rather by residence in the same community. Household and neighborhood social networks are again defined by address: sharing an address implies network connections. While, clearly, part of each individual's social network can be identified geographically, these network measurements are weak proxies in the sense that they also include many individuals who are not part of each other's social network. Yet there are observable social network effects even in social networks defined by geography.

Second, the social citizen plays a key role in elite political participation. Campaigns are increasingly attempting to employ social pressure to garner support for particular candidates, as exemplified by the My.BarackObama.com website, which allows people to form friendship groups or to invite friends to participate in online social networking. Campaigns have tapped into individual social networks. Friends motivate friends to donate to campaigns; these are very public interactions, with over 80 percent of all donations made in person at campaign events. In this instance, networks are defined both by shared behavior (donating to the same campaign) and by geography (living in the same congressional district). These networks are unique in that they are both politically and socially determined. Surveys of the donors indicate that shared behavior and, again, geography are weak proxies for an individual's social network, but at a minimum, individuals are likely to know their codonors. Interviews of the donors further suggest that they are influenced by their social networks.

Third, the social citizen can influence which candidate a voter chooses in a presidential election. Motivating a Democrat to vote for a Republican candidate or vice versa occurs over the course of a campaign and is more likely to occur in close relationships, either because of a family relationship or because of frequent interaction. This finding is based on two distinct national probability sample surveys, the second incorporating a panel data structure. Asking individuals about their specific networks is a completely different process than relying upon shared geography or shared behaviors. Yet, again, network effects emerge, and again, these networks appear to affect behavior.

Finally, the social citizen can influence the choice of party identification. The same correlation between discussant and respondent is present but can be seen to result, over time, in an unwillingness to acknowledge a party identification if there is a difference. As party identification is the single largest predictor of candidate choice, the social citizen here plays a particularly significant role. However, if social pressure is the primary mechanism and close relationships are likely to have greater influences, then, again, the social citizen is most likely to have influence within close relationships.

Social networks are measured in four distinct ways across in the chapters of this book. A number of different strategies were employed to ascertain the effects of these networks, ranging from randomized field experiments to interviews to modeling the selection process. Across all strategies and measurements, social network effects emerge. These networks influence fundamental political behaviors in American democracy.

The Evidence for Social Pressure

There are two underlying theoretical models of how political behavior is driven by social networks—one that assumes providing information influences behavior and one that holds that behavior is motivated by social influence. The social network effects presented here do not necessarily support one mechanism over the other, but they do suggest that individuals rely upon social networks to learn the social norms of political behavior and that some of these norms are sustained by explicit social pressure.

There is a tension between models that assume influence is achieved by providing information and those that assume influence is achieved through social pressure. For example, consider the standard model of the calculus of voting, which considers benefits, pivotality, costs, and civic duty. A voter's social network decreases costs (Downs 1957), as voters are able to rely upon trusted sources as information shortcuts (voters are also able to directly reduce costs via social networks by carpooling to polling places, for example). Yet social pressure enters the calculus of voting through a different component: the perception of civic duty (e.g., Gerber, Green, and Larimer 2008). The strongest evidence in this book that is directly attributable to a shift in perception of civic duty is presented in the second half of the second chapter, where it is shown that neighbors are more effective at door-to-door mobilization canvassing than strangers, even though both types of canvassers deliver an identical message—that is, information is held constant. Each subsequent chapter also finds empirical evidence consistent with a social conformity mechanism.

Social pressure is most effective when political behavior is publicly visible, as in voting. There is increased compliance with the social norm of voting when an individual resides with someone who has internalized that social norm. The postcards mailed in the experiment described in the second chapter were more effective when the recipient lived with a housemate who regularly turned out to participate. It is possible to imagine that these housemates participate at higher rates because they have internalized the social norm of voting. When recipients receive a postcard revealing their lack of participation, they are more likely to experience some dissonance if they reside with a voter who believes in the social norm of voting but they themselves have not been voting. In these cases, the recipient is more likely to cast a ballot than a recipient who lives with a housemate who seldom participates. To further support this possibility, the second chapter presents an experiment in which requests to participate delivered from neighbors were found to be more efficacious than requests from strangers. It is possible that increased levels of supervision from friends make an individual more susceptible to social pressure. It is also possible that individuals are simply more likely to help out a neighbor as part of their social obligations and that this kind of compliance to a social norm of participation does not need supervision. Social and civic responsibilities with respect to political participation frequently overlap and are difficult to distinguish. The survey data analysis supports the hypothesis of social influence as well. Geographically proximate network ties appear to have greater effects on candidate choice. Greater influence also correlates with closer relationships (such as those with family and those with friends with whom one has more frequent conversations). Individuals who interact more frequently are more likely to behave similarly.

There are no heterogeneous effects resulting from an individual's level of education—that is, individuals do not experience greater or lesser effects depending on their need for information. Varying the messenger—whether a neighbor or a stranger delivers the same information—should not determine the degree of the treatment effect if social influence is determined by shared information. Yet if social influence is determined by social pressure, a neighbor should have a greater effect than a stranger. The data presented here do not provide conclusive evidence that social pressure is the dominant mechanism driving social network effects, but they are highly suggestive that social pressure plays an important role, particularly since the effects are remarkably consistent across different political behaviors and different types of analysis.

Individuals are surely influenced by political information in their political behaviors. They are also likely influenced by trusted information—that is, information delivered to them specifically by a social network member. The studies described in the foregoing chapters establish that social pressure also plays a role in political behavior. A voter's social environment can influence political behavior through many channels. The evidence presented here demonstrates that social pressure is an important channel for social network effects. Unraveling the role of a citizen's social life in her political decisions is particularly critical in light of recent experimental findings in social psychology about the role of descriptive social norms in motivating behavioral choices such as recycling (Shultz 1999), water conservation (Cialdini 2009), and theft of natural resources (Cialdini 2003). These findings arise from a value-belief-norm model of human behavior (Stern et al. 1999). Social norms appear to be particularly effective at changing other nonpolitical behaviors, and linking the literature to this effect to the literature of political norms and behaviors (and evaluating the extent to which social pressure is involved) has the potential to inform political science.

Where Is Dahl's Ideal Democracy?

What are the social foundations of a participatory democracy? Democratic government is characterized by responsiveness to participatory citizens who, ideally, should have equal opportunities to form their preferences and to express those preferences in equal weight with the preferences of others (Dahl 1989). Participation in an ideal democracy indirectly leads to representation of sincere, individual preferences. Yet individuals do not form their preferences in isolation. Citizens form preferences in a social environment. While we typically consider individuals to be generally influenced by their friends and family, we seldom characterize a citizen as a product of the social environment. Canonical approaches attend only to individuals' resources or costs (Downs 1957; Olson 1965; Verba et al. 1995). The research in this book demonstrates that, instead, social environment determines individuals' political choices and participation.

Why does the social citizen play such a large role in participatory democracy? People are inherently social, and they place a high value on personal relationships. But they put little effort into becoming politically informed. Groups are most likely to survive when they are homogeneous, and thus individuals are most interested in maintaining their group membership and least interested in the political activities of the present. Consequently, individuals identify the political norms of their group and follow them, whether this involves donating money to campaigns, turning out to vote, or espousing particular political beliefs.

Typically, citizens of democratic governance have to aggregate their preferences through direct democracy, by voting for candidates or supporting interest groups. In an ideal democracy this occurs in isolation from others. Classical political science mostly assumes an individual citizen. Preference aggregation is largely considered exogenous to the social network: individuals are influenced by the media, mobilized by parties, and wooed by candidates. But what if individuals instead aggregate preferences in an endogenous way? That is, what if citizens influence each other? The concerns of classical political science are that this would result in a sort of mob rule, where self-governance is not possible and individuals are no longer given equal voice.

Yet while an ideal democracy is focused on preference formation and preference expression, participation does more than allow citizens to express preferences. In particular, it endows individuals with a sense of empowerment and a connection to government. Democracy involves more than elections. In particular, we need the social citizen to help resolve the collective action problems inherent in participatory democracy. Whether by reciprocity, reputation, or simply making a behavior publicly visible, the social citizen encourages her network to participate. A primary strategy that consistently emerged from the interviews with political donors was leveraging social ties to encourage a political action. Leveraging social ties ensures that there is enough participation for a functioning democratic system.

Consider once again the standard model of the calculus of voting as an example of the role of the social citizen. In this model, a citizen is a "better" citizen if she becomes more informed about the potential benefits of participating in elections, and she can accomplish this goal by independently acquiring political information or by communicating with trusted sources. Yet this outcome is in stark contrast to the consequences of a society of social citizens. A social citizen's network may convey either positive or negative social pressure about voting and other social norms, but she does not necessarily become a "better" citizen through these communications. That is, the quality of her vote is not necessarily positively affected by her social network. She may turn out to vote and cast a fully uninformed ballot. Worse still for an idealized democracy, she may be influenced to cast a ballot for a candidate that, were she voting in isolation, she would not support. The mechanism by which this social citizen is influenced may also be quite subtle. Social influence does not require obedience to an authority. Citizens are free to accept or decline requests from neighbors, family members, and friends; they are not coerced to participate. Yet, the desire for social conformity and harmonious social relationships is so great that there may not even be explicit requests for social conformity to take place. That this conformity occurs with respect to political norms has implications for our understanding of social networks and the fundamental civic responsibilities of citizens.

Social networks change the ways in which citizens interact in a civic society. On one hand, social interactions have a potentially deleterious effect on individual choice, and social networks affect choice in two key ways: social networks affect individuals' party identification and their candidate choice (which means that candidate choice is essentially affected twice). Individuals elect representatives who mirror a combination of their own preferences and the preferences of those around them. Yet individuals would be unlikely to turn out to vote for these representatives were it not for social ties. Without social connections, individuals would never learn the social norms of political participation. They would not appreciate that one of their civic responsibilities is to turn out to vote in an election. They would not fund campaigns. This would leave elections and candidates in the hands of an elite who might not necessarily represent the preferences of the typical citizen.

A Single Social Citizen

A single individual actually has more influence than simply one vote—as a member of a social society, each individual has the potential to influence members of her social network. Each individual has the potential to become the social citizen. Individuals follow others who speak passionately and forthrightly to their social network. Network members are attuned to sincerity; they do not mimic others thoughtlessly. Yet with sincere expression about a social political norm, it is possible to change behavior.

There are perils to a connected society. As voters are increasingly able to maintain geographically distant friendships (which the survey data from the 2000 ANES validate, as more than 40 percent of individuals have close relationships with partisan discussants who do not live in the same city), voters are more able to select discussants who share their socioeconomic and demographic characteristics—variables that are typically associated with political preferences. Political networks are likely to experience further change with the technological advances of this century. In February 2004 the Pew Internet and American Life Project conducted a survey on social ties in America. The report on the results of this survey finds that "traditional orientation to neighborhood- and village-based groups is moving towards communities that are oriented around geographically dispersed social networks" (Rainie,

Horrigan, and Cornfield 2005, 2). The Pew results also indicate that respondents were likely to get advice from people online. Many claim that Americans are increasingly "bowling alone" (Putnam 2000) and replacing neighborhood social interactions with online social interactions (Sunstein 2001). The Internet and other technological developments, such as nationwide long-distance cellular phone plans, change the people with whom each voter interacts. Thus individuals are less likely to be exposed to a politically diverse community. This lack of community diversity has the potential to produce polarized candidates who can target specific communities without having to appeal to a broad audience. This book suggests that institutions that increase dialogue across ideological lines could produce a more informed electorate and better representation . Yet only those networks that include socially close relationships are likely to have significant effects.

Researchers have long observed that individuals behave similarly to those who share their socioeconomic and demographic characteristics. This book demonstrates one explanation of this fact, which is that individuals are likely to form friendships with those who are like them and to share behaviors within those friendship networks. Small changes in partisanship or vote choice based on political network communication can have broad effects across the entire electorate, resulting in many small correlations within each network. A social citizen can affect positive change simply by voicing normative preferences within her social network. This can increase voter turnout, ensure candidates are funded locally, or change the political preferences of the electorate. These changes can be brought about most efficaciously within the most personal and intimate relationships. These social connections are part of our inherent human sociability. How socially connected are we? If our political behavior is linked across networks, then the distribution of our close friends and relationships, across the country, has the potential to dictate democratic outcomes.

Notes

1. Of the 1,066 individuals who responded to the question "Do you ever discuss politics with your family and friends?" 850 individuals responded "yes" in the 2004 ANES.

2. One alternative, not discussed here, is that individuals may also be influenced via an internal channel, having personally embraced a social norm. An example of the resulting socialized behavior is that individuals, upon entering an elevator, all face toward the elevator door. While these internal norms are consequences of social learning, they have little to do with the influence exerted by an individual's social ties, as politics become a salient group characteristic.

3. Models that assume these two different methods of link formation produce different theoretical predictions about the resulting shape of the network (Jackson and Rogers 2007).

4. Huckfeldt and Sprague (1987, 1988) and Huckfeldt, Sprague, and Levine (2000) conducted snowball surveys, in which they asked respondents to identify political discussion partners and then surveyed the discussion partners. Unfortunately, only nonrelatives were considered political discussion partners. The General Social Survey (GSS) included a social network battery in 1987 and 1988. The 2000 ANES included a network battery, and the 2004 ANES asked respondents whether they ever discuss politics with their family or friends and how often that discussion occurs. The fields of both political science and sociology have benefited from inclusion of survey questions regarding details of a respondent's political network. The GSS social network battery produced

innovations in the analysis of network survey data (Marsden 1990), increasing understanding of the structure of political discussion networks (Marsden 1987) and of the relationship between organizational affiliations and network density (Liedka 1991). The GSS provided researchers with data to analyze with whom people discuss politics, the frequency of that discussion, and the impact of political discussion on political participation (Straits 1991; Knoke 1990).

5. They used a two-stage instrument in which they first surveyed a set of individuals and then surveyed a subset of the people with whom these individuals said they had discussed politics. They were interested in the content of "socially transmitted political information" (468) and specifically how majority and minority preferences are shaped by social context. They interviewed approximately fifteen hundred respondents in their initial survey, which asked for the names of "three people you talked with most about the events of the past election year." If no name was generated, the survey then asked respondents to provide names of people "with whom you were most likely to have informal conversations during the course of the past few months" (468). A follow-up survey of these names produced 950 interviews with discussion partners.

6. Huckfeldt and Sprague (1988) argue that "when a citizen considers whether to discuss politics regularly with another individual, the choice is predicated upon her agreement or disagreement with the potential discussant. If agreement is present, the person is accepted as a discussant, but if disagreement is present then the citizen must either look for a new discussant or accept a politically disagreeable discussant and, hence, a politically dissonant relationship" (470). They also note that "people living among Republicans, ceteris paribus, have fewer opportunities to choose political discussants who support Mondale" (470).

7. In particular, sociologists have posited that individuals are influenced by the preferences of their strongest social ties (Cooley 1912; Newcomb 1943; Lazarsfeld, Berelson, and Gaudet 1948). Human relationships can be broadly classified into secondary groups, with weak social ties, and primary groups, with strong social ties. These preferences may be political.

8. Research by Huckfeldt, Johnson, and Sprague (2004) has documented that individuals are well aware of the political preferences of their network.

9. Weatherford uses ANES data in the aggregate to examine variables that may affect local political networks, including the number of years an individual has been a resident in her house, whether or not the individual is locally employed, whether or not the individual shops locally and attends a local church, and the quality of the individual's neighborhood. Weatherford also includes a set of individual social and political characteristics (socioeconomic status, political interest, party affiliation, and ideology) as well as a set of variables that affect the degree of social interaction with local residents (duration of friendships, frequency of contact). Weatherford then estimates linear regression coefficients for all of these variables using a series of dependent variables that are "network properties," such as politicization and party similarity.

10. Other scholars have made similar claims about the role of social networks in models of participation. James Coleman (1988) demonstrates that if it is socially beneficial for everyone to participate and individuals are linked

together, then people will participate when they would not have as individuals. Other authors (Sheingold 1973; Putnam 1966) have also suggested that voting should be considered in the framework of social interactions. Putnam describes "social interaction theory" as follows: "Community influence is mediated primarily through the numerous personal contacts among members of a community. Such social interaction within the community would, on the whole, tend to support political attitudes commonly held by community members, and to undermine 'deviant views' " (641). Putnam finds that "community influence is to a considerable extent mediated through friendship groups" (649). Social interactions are valuable cues for predicting voting patterns.

CHAPTER 2

1. In Los Angeles County, local businesses even occasionally offer discounts to people wearing the "I VOTED" stickers to encourage citizens to fulfill their civic responsibilities. Explained one Los Angeles County Krispy Kreme doughnut shop owner, "We can't guarantee that your candidate of preference will win on Nov. 4, but we can guarantee that your right to voice your choice will be rewarded with a patriotic doughnut that will remind you just how tasty freedom really is" (Chang 2008).

2. That these effects are difficult to identify is well established in the literature on social networks, and this problem is typically driven by the presence of homophily and shared context. Shalizi and Thomas (2010) describe the inferential complications resulting from homophily and shared context. They are difficult to overcome without either additional statistical techniques such as sensitivity analysis (VanderWeele and Arah 2010) or different research design strategies such as conducting randomized field experiments.

3. Other scholars have examined spillover effects in contexts unrelated to political behavior (Duflo and Saez 2003; Munshi 2004; Besley and Case 1993).

4. Rahm Emanuel had previously held the seat but resigned to become the White House chief of staff. Twenty-four candidates competed in the March 3 special election primary. Three candidates emerged to compete in the April 7 special election: Mike Quigley (Democrat), Rosanna Pulido (Republican) and Matt Reichel (Green). Michael Quigley won the election, receiving 69.2 percent of the 44,138 votes.

5. The Republican Party did very little campaigning for Pulido, who is a founder of the Illinois branch of the anti-illegal-immigration group known as the Minutemen (Isenstadt 2009).

6. No more than one individual in each household received the postcard. The study was also restricted to nine-digit zip codes containing at least two households with two eligible individuals and somewhere between three and fifteen total households.

7. For further details on the random assignment, see Sinclair, McConnell, and Green (2010).

8. The postcard was mailed April 2, 2009, and most residents received the postcard on either April 3 or April 4, 2009, three or four days before the election.

9. Details of the analysis can be found in the full text of Sinclair, McConnell, and Green (2010).

10. Another explanation that reconciles this small effect with the standard theories about mobilization spillover and eliminates the need for communication between individuals is shame. Individuals might receive the postcard and not wish to share the message with other individuals because they do not want others to know they have violated a social norm. That is, a voter who has not participated in previous spring elections does not share the information on the postcard with other members in her household. Individuals who had voted in both previous elections that would more likely have communicated about the treatment to other members of their household, whereas individuals who had voted in neither of the previous elections would more likely have failed to communicate the treatment with other members of their household. A regression analysis of the household spillover effects separating the population by voting history tests to see if there are any differences based upon previous vote history. In this analysis, the coefficient for household spillover in two-person households where the treated individual voted in both previous elections is .0305 with a standard error of .0210, and in two-person households where the treated individual voted in neither of the previous elections, the coefficient for household spillover is .0095 with a standard error of .0109. Not only do the 95 percent confidence intervals of these coefficients overlap, but furthermore, neither coefficient is statistically distinguishable from zero. The pattern is also true for three-person households. Shame is unlikely to be the mechanism generating the null effects. There is also no evidence to support a mechanism of mimicry: the fact that one individual in a household or neighborhood is more likely to vote does not imply that others will necessarily follow. This is particularly surprising given that the treatment had both a large direct effect and that other household members likely could observe the treatment in the mail.

11. The experiment randomly assigned 11,789 individuals to be included in the treatment category and 3,578 individuals to be included in the control category. A canvasser—either a local or a nonlocal—tried to contact each individual who was assigned to the treatment category. Of those assigned to treatment, 45 percent were successfully contacted over the course of the four-week campaign. Additional details of the experiment are available in Sinclair, McConnell, and Michelson (2010).

12. We also estimated the power of local canvassing without the outlier where the share of local contacts was greater than 50 percent. The strong positive relationship persists. This observational analysis confirms that being contacted by a local canvasser has a significant impact on the probability of voting.

CHAPTER 3

1. This is according to the Center for Responsive Politics, http://www
.opensecrets.org/bigpicture/instvsout.php?cycle=2008. Additionally, the district includes four of the top ten donating zip codes in the state, corresponding to the towns of Winnetka, Lake Forest, Highland Park, and Glencoe. The Win-

netka zip code had the eighteenth-highest amount of political contributions in the United States.

2. The median housing unit value is $370,080. There are approximately seven hundred thousand residents in this congressional district, of which a large majority are white (83 percent) and highly educated (92 percent have at least a high school degree and 50 percent have at least a bachelors degree).

3. By far, a majority of the Tenth District representatives have been Republican. Representative Mark Kirk's predecessor was another moderate Republican, John Porter, who served for over twenty years. Typically, Porter won over 65 percent of the vote in his congressional elections. In his final election, he ran unopposed. The district's last Democratic representative was Abner Mikva, who went on to serve on the US Court of Appeals from 1975 to 1979. The Republican legacy began with Elihu Washburne, who was a founder of the Republican Party, a close advisor to President Abraham Lincoln, and secretary of state for President Ulysses Grant.

4. These contributors made 1,091 contributions (4 percent of all contributions), an average of 3.9 contributions per contributor. The mean contribution from Sheridan Road was $1,349.15, and the median amount was $500.

5. Zip codes corresponding with the towns listed on Illinois Tenth District Representative Kirk's website were used to determine which zip codes were eligible. Because of campaign contribution limits and administrative blunders, negative gifts were included in the database. These negative amounts were subtracted from the same individuals' positive donations to the same organization. Additionally, data from the FEC are registered by individuals, and there are frequently inconsistencies in the first name or profession for the same individual, as some use a nickname or different job titles for the same position. Individuals were identified as a the same donor if there was a match in their last name and their first name, middle name, or employer were the same.

6. The results reported in this chapter were evaluated for consistency when this variable was replaced with the Zillow estimate for the current appraisal value of the house that corresponded to the family's address. The results reported in this section are robust to the Zillow data. For zip codes 60065, 60070, and 60094, the census variable was not available. This may be the result of donors' errors when reporting their zip code to the FEC or of areas being too small or otherwise not analyzed specifically by the US Census Bureau. Nine individuals from these zip codes were coded as having missing information for all of the statistics from the 2000 Census.

7. There is a large right tail to the distribution of gift amounts: the mean donation was $1,069 with a standard deviation of $2,356.63, although there are fewer and fewer gifts at higher amounts. Interestingly, this trend is clearly broken at the points where donors can "max out": at the $2,300 and $4,600 donation amounts. As $2,300 is the limit for campaign contributions to a specific candidate for primary or general elections and $4,600 is the limit for the entire election cycle, 4,321 donations were made for $2,300 and 122 donations for $4,600.

8. There is no easy way to describe the group of political organizations that had ten or fewer donations; among them are organizations for lesser-known

out-of-district politicians (e.g., David Woods for Congress), committees to elect other states' candidates (e.g., Indiana Republican State Committee, Inc.), PACs focused on obscure political issues (e.g., Fraternity and Sorority Political Action Committee), and PACs focused on specific industries or companies (e.g., Tile Industry and TTX Company Employees PACs). The remaining political organizations had higher-profile PACs or candidate campaigns and receive many more donations. The organizations that received the most donations (and were consequently quite representative of all the organizations in the second group) were Obama for America with 6,402 gifts, Kirk for Congress with 2,456 gifts, Dan Seals for Congress with 1,976 gifts, and John McCain 2008, Inc., with 1,773 gifts.

9. The ages averaged here reflect the donor age in 2008. In other words, a donor's age was calculated by subtracting the donor's birth year from 2008.

10. The two outliers—donors with gifts over $150,000—are excluded from this analysis, as these are gifts from candidates to themselves. However, the results are robust to the inclusion of these data points.

11. Negative binomial regression is appropriate because the dependent variable is a count variable.

12. The survey question read, "Below is a list of other residents in your congressional district. Please circle the names of individuals that you have met at least once. Your answers will be kept confidential and will be used solely for research purposes."

13. Similar results are generated using an indicator coded 1 if the respondent indicated that either their immediate family give or that their friends give and coded 0 if she indicated otherwise.

14. According to the FEC website (http://www.fec.gov), "A contribution is 'made' on the date when you relinquish control over it. If mailed, a contribution is 'made' on the date of the postmark."

15. The survey question is worded, "Please describe why you make campaign contributions."

16. The survey question is worded, "Do you think you have influenced other people to contribute to campaigns and political organizations? Whom have you influenced and how have you done so?"

17. In 1984, a year in which the general contribution rate was 10.7 percent, the ANES asked how they were solicited. Among those asked to contribute in a mailing, 8.9 percent did contribute and cited the mailing as the cause. Among those asked to contribute with a telephone call, 21 percent did and cited the telephone call as the cause. Among those asked face-to-face to contribute, 39 percent did and cited that personal contact as the cause. This high rate of donation after personal contact recruitment is extremely consistent with the other findings in this chapter.

CHAPTER 4

1. These data are based on responses to the following: "We hear a lot of talk these days about liberals and conservatives. Here is a seven-point scale on which the political views that people might hold are arranged from

extremely liberal to extremely conservative. Where would you place yourself on this scale, or haven't you thought much about this?" The totals are
244 Democratic voters who self-identified as liberals, 135 Democratic voters
who self-identifiedas conservatives, 341 Republican voters who self-identified
as liberals, 394 Republican voters who self-identified as conservatives, and
62 nonresponses. The first of the two studies discussed in this chapter focuses
on self-reported ideology, while the second focuses on self-reported party identification. This strategy is employed to ensure the robustness of the perceived
phenomena.

2. This is the "reflection" problem, where trying to determine the causal
mechanism of an individual with a group is "similar to the problem of interpreting the almost simultaneous movements of a person and his reflection in a
mirror. Does the mirror image cause the person's movements or reflect them?
An observer who does not understand something of optics and human behavior would not be able to tell" (Manski 1993, 129).

3. It should be noted here that "switching" is not the particular focus
of this chapter, but rather the influences of the discussion network on the
respondent's candidate choices. "Switchers" are simply discussed as examples
of motivation.

4. Respondents' choice of political networks may be related to observed
characteristic of the voter. Specifically, voters select a neighborhood and a
social group based upon their own characteristics (children, marriage, gender,
race, etc.), and these variables may also be associated with particular political
ideologies. For example, a respondent's reported discussion partner's political
ideology is highly correlated with her own (Huckfeldt, Johnson, and Sprague
2004; Mutz 2006).

5. For a review of this literature and the Columbia School findings, see
Eulau 1980.

6. The General Social Survey completed a social network battery in 1987
and 1988, but there is little to identify networks' political ideology or respondents' political ideology. The 2004 ANES asked respondents if they ever
discuss politics with their family or friends and the frequency with which that
discussion occurs. However, these questions do not address the partisan nature
of the discussants, which plays a crucial role in determining the respondents'
preferences and information set. The ANES provided data from which to
analyze with whom people discuss politics, the frequency of that discussion,
and the impact of political discussion on political participation (Straits 1991;
Knoke 1990). The ANES social network battery led to an increased understanding of the relationship between disagreement and social ties (Huckfeldt,
Johnson, and Sprague 2004).

7. Surveys often ask for discussants of "important matters." There are mini-
mal differences between these two name-generators (Klofstad, McClurg, and
Rolfe 2009).

8. Nine percent of the 346 individuals who had the same partisan preferences were misidentified, and 36.5 percent of the 219 individuals who had
different partisan preferences were misidentified (1035).

9. For an example of such an effect, see Nickerson (2008).

10. For a potential way to address these criticisms methodologically in the context of rich network data, see Christakis and Fowler 2008.

11. The 2000 ANES data are provided by the Interuniversity Consortium for Political and Social Research. Congressional district returns for the 2000 presidential election were provided by Gary Jacobson.

12. Respondents were prompted to provide discussants by the following script: "From time to time, people discuss government, elections and politics with other people. I'd like to ask you about the people with whom you discuss these matters. These people might or might not be relatives. Can you think of anyone?" Then they were asked about their discussants' choices and actions: "How do you think NAME1 voted in the election? Do you think he/she voted for Al Gore, George Bush, some other candidate, or do you think NAME1 didn't vote?"

13. The questions include evaluating Asians, feminists, Protestants, Jews, Catholics, the Christian Coalition, homosexuals, the environment, older people, women, fundamentalist Christians, Hispanics, welfare recipients, the poor, big business, labor unions, liberals, conservatives, whites, blacks, the federal government, the military, Congress, the Supreme Court, George H. W. Bush, Jesse Jackson, Ralph Nader, Bill Clinton, Republicans in the House, Democrats in the House, Al Gore, and George W. Bush.

14. Individuals were removed from the data set if their discussion network was evenly split between Republicans and Democrats, as it was then impossible to determine the majority party. Thus 126 individuals were dropped from the analyses.

15. It is similarly possible to tabulate the Bush vote while examining only the majority-party discussion network. The greatest percentage of Bush votes came from individuals who report having an all-Republican discussion network. Individuals who reported having a mixed-party discussion network fall into the middle category, and individuals who report having an all-Democratic discussion network fall into the lowest category.

16. Analysis with indicators for missing observations generates nearly identical results.

17. First differences were calculated using Clarify (Tomz, Wittenberg, and King 2001).

18. As stated in the CCAP Codebook, "YouGov/Polimetrix constructed a sampling frame for CCAP from the 2005–7 American Community Survey (ACS), including data on age, race, gender, education, marital status, number of children under 18, family income, employment status, citizenship, state, and metropolitan area. The frame was constructed by stratified sampling from the full 2005–7 ACS sample with selection within strata by weighted sampling with replacements (using the person weights on the public use file). Data on reported 2008 voter registration and turnout from the November 2008 Current Population Survey Supplement was matched to this frame using a weighted Euclidean distance metric. Data on religion, church attendance, born again or evangelical status, news interest, party identification and ideology was matched from the 2007 Pew Religious Life Survey. The target sample was selected by stratification on age, race, gender, education, and state (with battleground

states double sampled) using simple random sampling within strata, excluding all non-registered persons" (Jackman and Vavreck. 2008, 1).

19. The survey reads, "From time to time, people discuss government, elections and politics with other people. I'd like to know the names of three people you talk with about these matters. Just tell me their first names or initials."

20. Those respondents who could name no discussants were dropped from future analysis. Seventy-two percent named three discussants, 4 percent named two discussants, 7 percent named one discussant, and 16 percent named zero discussants.

21. These groups are not mutually exclusive. Also, less than 1 percent of all discussants were described by the respondent as an "advisor." Almost 4 percent of all discussants were classified as Internet-based relationships.

22. Respondents' political ideology was assessed in two other ways, and the results are robust by either method. First, the respondent's five-point ideology was used, ranging from very liberal to very conservative. Second, a more nuanced measurement may also be needed than the seven-point scale of self-reported partisanship or five-point scale of self-reported ideology. For this analysis, a one-dimensional latent utility score was constructed for each respondent to be used as an ideology proxy. This variable was constructed using a series of policy questions on the survey, which include opinions on abortion, immigration, gay marriage, health care policy, Iraq, and the environment.

23. Results with all covariates are shown tables 4.6 and 4.8 in the appendix. These covariates include gender, race, marital status, education level, employment status, and income. Variation in sample size is due to missing data on the dependent variable.

24. After postprocessing, the coefficient for this indicator variable is .22, standard deviation .028. First differences for this variable, moving from having a majority of network members not supporting Obama to a majority supporting Obama, would increase the probability of an Obama vote by 61 percent.

CHAPTER 5

1. Eight individuals who identified as liberal or very liberal also identified as at least leaning Republican, and forty-one individuals who identified as conservative or very conservative identified themselves as at least leaning Democratic. Together, these individuals account for approximately 5 percent of the 1,026 respondents.

2. Polimetrix surveyed approximately one hundred thirty-three thousand individuals from the last week of September through the first Tuesday in November 2006 and provided a random sample of one thousand individuals who answered this particular battery, matched by covariates to the 2004 American Community Survey (ACS). Although the survey population by itself would likely be different than a random sample, as Internet users tend to have higher income and education levels, comparison with the 2004 ACS by one-to-one matching does provide the equivalent of a random sample.

3. See the appendix to this chapter for detailed question wording.

4. This classification by definition treats partisanship unequally, weighing

Democratic discussion partners more heavily (suppose that an individual had one Republican discussion partner and one Democratic discussion partner, for example).

5. The following variables are incomplete from the set of 781 observations: ideological self-placement (747 responses), income (631 responses), education level (780 responses), geographic distance of first discussant (765 responses), geographic distance of second discussant (737 responses), frequency of conversation with the first discussant (769 responses), frequency of conversation with the second discussant (738 responses), method of communication with the first discussant (768 responses), method of communication with the second discussant (738 responses), and frequency with which the discussants participate in national elections (743 responses).

6. The missing variables are likely missing at random. They are correlated with other observations in the data set, and thus Amelia is appropriate. Producing multiple data sets helps eliminate any bias that would be introduced as a consequence of the imputation (King et al. 2001).

7. There is overall improvement in balance but the covariates will still be included as control variables and the matching will be used as a preprocessing technique for the data. The percentage overall improvement in covariates as a result of matching for each data set—the covariates, on average, look more similar for the two types of discussant groups. Many of the covariates themselves, however, show enormous percentage decreases in improvement, in particular the geographic distance from the first discussant, if the discussants are group members, and the principle method of communication with the first discussant. Because not every covariate demonstrates improvement in distance across treatment groups, the covariates will still be included as control variables and the matching will be used as a preprocessing technique for the data (Ho et al. 2007a, 2007b).

8. The standard errors were adjusted appropriately, as the models were fit using Zelig (Imai, King, and Lau 2006).

9. The equivalent result for ordinary least squares using the three-point party identification measurement would have a mean of $-.337$, a standard deviation of .059, and an N of 2,934. Equivalent results for Democratic, independent, and Republican identifications for the ordered logit would have means of .177 (sd .09), $-.02$ (sd .1551), and $-.155$ (sd .09), respectively.

10. This name-generator is similar to that used by Huckfeldt and Sprague in their St. Louis–Indianapolis survey (1996) and was later applied to the 2000 ANES. Huckfeldt and Sprague demonstrated that there was no difference in responses between this question and an equivalent question which asked people about "important" matters. The questions which follow in this survey are unique.

Works Cited

Abrajano, Marisa, and Costas Panagopoulos. 2009. "Does Language Matter? The Impact of Spanish- versus English-Language GOTV Efforts on Latino Turnout." Unpublished manuscript.

Abramowitz, Alan I. 1983. "Social Determinism, Rationality, and Partisanship among College Students." *Political Behavior* 5 (4): 353–62.

Abramowitz, Alan I., and Kyle L. Saunders. 1998. "Ideological Realignment in the U.S. Electorate." *Journal of Politics* 60 (3): 634–52.

Abramson, Paul R., John H. Aldrich, and David W. Rohde. 1998. *Change and Continuity in the 1996 Elections*. Washington, DC: CQ Press.

Achen, Christopher H. 1992. "Social Psychology, Demographic Variables, and Linear Regression: Breaking the Iron Triangle in Voting Research." *Political Behavior* 14:195–211.

———. 2002. "Parental Socialization and Rational Party Identification." *Political Behavior* 24 (2): 141–70.

Aizer, Anna, and Janet Currie. 2004. "Networks or Neighborhoods? Interpreting Correlations in the Use of Publicly-Funded Maternity Care in California." *Journal of Public Economics* 88 (12): 2573–85.

Alford, John, Carolyn Funk, and John R. Hibbing. 2005. "Are Political Orientations Genetically Transmitted?" *American Journal of Political Science* 99 (2): 601–13.

Allen, V. L. 1965. "Situational Factors in Conformity." In *Advances in Experimental Social Psychology*, edited by Leonard Berkowitz, vol. 2, 133–76. New York: Academic.

Almond, Gabriel A., and Sidney Verba. 1963. *The Civic Culture: Political Attitudes and Democracy in Five Nations*. Princeton, NJ: Princeton University Press.

Alvarez, R. Michael. 1998. *Information and Elections*. Ann Arbor: University of Michigan Press.

Alvarez, R. Michael, and John Brehm. 2002. *Hard Choices, Easy Answers: Values, Information, and American Public Opinion*. Princeton, NJ: Princeton University Press.

Alvarez, R. Michael, and Jonathan Nagler. 1998. "When Politics and Models Collide: Estimating Models of Multi-Party Elections." *American Journal of Political Science* 42 (1): 55–96.

———. 2000. "A New Approach for Modeling Strategic Voting in Multiparty Elections." *British Journal of Political Science* 30 (1): 57–75.

Andreoni, James. 1988. "Privately Provided Public Goods in a Large Economy: The Limits of Altruism." *Journal of Public Economics* 35: 57–73.

———. 1989. "Giving with Impure Altruism: Applications to Charity and Ricardian Equivalence." *Journal of Political Economy* 97: 1447–58.

Andreoni, James, and B. Douglas Bernheim. 2009. "Social Image and the 50–50 Norm: A Theoretical and Experimental Analysis of Audience Effects." *Econometrica* 77 (5): 1607–36.

Ansolabehere, Stephen, John M. deFigueiredo, and James M. Snyder. 2003. "Why Is There So Little Money in U.S. Politics?" *Journal of Economic Perspectives* 17 (1): 105–30.

Ansolabehere, Stephen, James M. Snyder Jr., and Charles Stewart III. 2000. "Old Voters, New Voters, and the Personal Vote: Using Redistricting to Measure the Incumbency Advantage." *American Journal of Political Science* 44:17–34.

———. 2001. "Candidate Positioning in U.S. House Elections." *American Journal of Political Science* 45 (1): 136–59.

"Aral, Sinan, Lev Muchnik, and Arun Sundararajan. 2009. "Distinguishing Influence-Based Contagion from Homophily Driven Diffusion in Dynamic Networks." *Proceedings of the National Academy of Sciences of the United States of America* 106 (51): 21544–49.

Asch, Solomon E. 1955. "Opinions and Social Pressure." *Scientific American* 193:31–35.

———. 1956. "Studies of Independence and Conformity: A Minority of One against a Unanimous Majority." *Psychological Monographs* 70 (9): 416.

———. 1963. "Effects of Group Pressure upon the Modification and Distortion of Judgments." In *Groups, Leadership and Men: Research in Human Relations*, ed. Harold Guetzkow, 177–90. New York: Russell and Russell.

Bartels, Larry M. 2008. *Unequal Democracy: The Political Economy of the New Gilded Age*. Princeton, NJ: Princeton University Press.

Baumeister, R. F., and M. R. Leary. 1995. "The Need to Belong: Desire for Interpersonal Attachments as a Fundamental Human Motive." *Psychological Bulletin* 117:497–529.

Baybeck, Brady. 2006. "Sorting out the Competing Effects of Racial Context." *Journal of Politics* 68 (2): 386–96.

Baybeck, Brady, and R. Robert Huckfeldt. 2002a. "Spatially Dispersed Ties among Interdependent Citizens: Connecting Individuals and Aggregates." *Political Analysis* 10 (3): 261–75.

———. 2002b. "Urban Contexts, Spatially Dispersed Networks, and the Diffusion of Political Information." *Political Geography* 21 (2): 195–220.

Beck, Paul, Russell J. Dalton, Steven Greene, and R. Robert Huckfeldt. 2002. "The Social Calculus of Voting: Interpersonal, Media, and Organizational Influences on Presidential Choices." *American Political Science Review* 96 (1): 57–74.

Bednar, Jenna, and Elisabeth R. Gerber. 2011. "Political Geography, Campaign Contributions, and Representation." University of Michigan working paper. http://www-personal.umich.edu/~jbednar/WIP/irod_050211_wfigs.pdf.

Belknap, George, and Angus Campbell. 1952. "Political Party Identification and Attitudes toward Foreign Policy." *Public Opinion Quarterly* 15 (4): 601–23.

Bellini, Luciana. 2008. "ObamaLand.com." *Seven Magazine*, November 20, 2008.

Bénabou, Roland, and Jean Tirole. 2006. "Incentives and Prosocial Behavior." *American Economic Review* 96 (5): 1652–78.

Berelson, Bernard R., Paul F. Lazarsfeld, and William N. McPhee. 1954. *Voting: A Study of Opinion Formation in a Presidential Campaign*. Chicago: University of Chicago Press.

Bergstrom, Ted, Lawrence Blume, and Hal Varian. 1986. "On the Private Provision of Public Goods." *Journal of Public Economics* 29 (1): 25–49.

Berman, Ari. 2008. "The Dean Legacy." *Nation*, February 28.

Besley, Timothy, and Anne Case. 1993. "Modeling Technology Adoption in Developing Countries." *American Economic Review* 83 (2): 396–402.

Blais, André. 2000. *To Vote or Not to Vote? The Merits and Limits of Rational Choice Theory*. Pittsburgh: University of Pittsburgh Press.

Bolsen, Toby. 2010. "A Light Bulb Goes On: Norms, Rhetoric, and Actions for the Public Good." Working manuscript.

Bolton, Charles. 1972. "Alienation and Action: A Study of Peace Group Members." *American Journal of Sociology* 78 (3): 537–61.

Bond, Michael Harris, and Peter B. Smith. 1996. "Cross-Cultural Social and Organizational Psychology." *Annual Review of Psychology* 47:205–35.

Boslaugh, Sarah E., Douglas A. Luke, Ross C. Brownson, Kimberly S. Naleid, and Matthew W. Kreuter. 2004. "Perceptions of Neighborhood Environment for Physical Activity: Is It 'Who You Are' or 'Where You Live'?" *Journal of Urban Health* 81 (4): 671–81.

Brady, Henry E., Kay Lehman Schlozman, and Sidney Verba. 1999. "Prospecting for Participants: Rational Expectations and the Recruitment of Political Activists." *American Political Science Review* 93 (1): 153–68.

Brady, Henry E., Sidney Verba, and Kay Lehman Schlozman. 1995. "Beyond SES: A Resource Model of Political Participation." *American Political Science Review* 89 (2): 271–95.

Brehm, Sharon S., and Jack W. Brehm. 1981. *Psychological Reactance: A Theory of Freedom and Control*. New York: Academic.

Briet, Martien, Bert Klandermans, and Frederike Kroon. 1987. "How Women Became Involved in the Women's Movement of the Netherlands." In *The Women's Movements of the United States and Western Europe: Consciousness, Political Opportunities, and Public Policy*, edited by Mary Katzenstein and Carol Mueller, 44–67. Philadelphia: Temple University Press.

Brody, Richard A., and Lawrence Rothenberg. 1988. "The Instability of Partisanship: An Analysis of the 1980 Presidential Election." *British Journal of Political Science* 18: 445–65.

Brown, Clifford W., Jr., Lynda W. Powell, and Clyde Wilcox. 1995. *Serious Money: Fundraising and Contributing in Presidential Nomination Campaigns*. New York: Cambridge University Press.

Campbell, Angus, Philip E. Converse, Warren Miller, and Donald Stokes. 1960. *The American Voter*. Chicago: University of Chicago Press.

Campbell, Angus, George Gurin, and Warren E. Miller. 1954. *The Voter Decides*. Evanston, IL: Row, Peterson.

Cassel, Carol A. 1983. "Predicting Party Identification, 1956–80: Who Are the Republicans and Who Are the Democrats?" *Political Behavior* 4 (3): 265–82.

Chang, Andrea. 2008. "Shops and Restaurants Elect to Offer Freebies to Voters Today." *Los Angeles Times*, November 4.

Chappell, Henry W., Jr. 1982. "Campaign Contributions and Congressional Voting: A Simultaneous Probit-Tobit Model." *Review of Economics and Statistics* 64 (1): 77–83.

Cho, Wendy K. Tam. 2003. "Contagion Effects and Ethnic Contribution Networks." *American Journal of Political Science* 47 (2): 368–87.

Cho, Wendy K. Tam, and James G. Gimpel. 2007. "Prospecting for (Campaign) Gold." *American Journal of Political Science* 51 (2): 255–68.

Cho, Wendy K. Tam, James G. Gimpel, and Joshua J. Dyck. 2006. "Residential Concentration, Political Socialization, and Voter Turnout." *Journal of Politics* 68 (1): 156–67.

———. 2010. "Rough Terrain: Spatial Variation in Campaign Contributing and Volunteerism." *American Journal of Political Science* 54 (1): 74–89.

Chong, Dennis. 1991. *Collective Action and the Civil Rights Movement*. Chicago: University of Chicago Press.

Christakis, Nicholas A., and James H. Fowler. 2007. "The Spread of Obesity in a Large Social Network over 32 Years." *New England Journal of Medicine* 357 (4): 370–79.

———. 2008. "The Collective Dynamics of Smoking in a Large Social Network." *New England Journal of Medicine* 358 (21): 2249–58.

———. 2009. *Connected: The Surprising Power of Our Social Networks and How They Shape Our Lives*. New York: Little, Brown.

Cialdini, Robert B. 2003. "Crafting Normative Messages to Protect the Environment." *Current Directions in Psychological Science* 12:105–9.

———. 2007. *Influence: The Psychology of Persuasion*. Rev. ed. New York: Collins Business.

———. 2009. *Influence: Science and Practice*. 5th ed. Boston: Pearson Education.

Cialdini, Robert B., and Noah J. Goldstein. 2004. "Social Influence: Compliance and Conformity." *Annual Review of Psychology* 55:591–621.

Cialdini, Robert B., and Melanie R. Trost. 1998. "Social Influence: Social Norms, Conformity and Compliance." In *The Handbook of Social Psychology*, 4th ed., edited by Daniel T. Gilbert, Susan T. Fiske, and Gardner Lindzey, 151–92. Hoboken, NJ: Wiley and Sons.

Cohen-Cole, Ethan, and Jason M. Fletcher. 2008. "Detecting Implausible Social Network Effects in Acne, Height, and Headaches: Longitudinal Analysis." *British Medical Journal* 10 (227): A2533.

Coleman, James S. 1958. "Relational Analysis: The Study of Social Organization with Survey Methods." *Human Organization* 17:28–36.

———. 1988. "Free Riders and Zealots: The Role of Social Networks." *Sociological Theory* 6 (1): 52–57.

Conover, Pamela Johnston, and Stanley Feldman. 1989. "Candidate Perception in an Ambiguous World: Campaigns, Cues, and Inference Processes." *American Journal of Political Science* 33 (4): 912–40.

Conover, Pamela Johnston, Ivor M. Crewe, and Donald D. Searing. 2002. "The Deliberative Potential of Political Discussion." *British Journal of Political Science* 32: 21–62.

Converse, Philip E. 1962. "Information Flow and the Stability of Partisan Attitudes." *Public Opinion Quarterly* 26 (4): 578–99.

———. 1964. "The Nature of Belief Systems in Mass Publics." In *Ideology and Discontent*, edited by David E. Apter. New York: Free Press.

———. 1966. "Information Flow and the Stability of Partisan Attitudes." In *Elections and the Political Order*, edited by Angus Campbell et al. New York: Wiley and Sons.

Cooley, C. H. 1912. *Social Organization*. New York: Charles Scribner's Sons.

Rainie, Lee, John Horrigan, and Michael Cornfield. 2005. "The Internet and Campaign 2004: A Look Back at the Campaigners." Pew Internet and American Life Project working paper. http://www.pewinternet.org/Reports/2005/The-Internet-and-Campaign-2004.aspx.

Cox, Gary W., Frances McCall Rosenbluth, and Michael F. Thies. 1998. "Mobilization, Social Networks, and Turnout: Evidence from Japan." *World Politics* 50 (3): 447–74.

Croson, Rachel, and Jen Shang. 2011. "Social Influences in Giving." In *The Science of Giving: Experimental Approaches to the Study of Charity*, edited by Daniel M. Oppenheimer and Christopher Y. Olivola, 65–80. New York: Psychology Press.

Dahl, Robert. 1971. *Polyarchy: Participation and Opposition*. New Haven, CT: Yale University Press.

———. 1989. *Democracy and Its Critics*. New Haven, CT: Yale University Press.

Dawes, Christopher T., James H. Fowler, Tim Johnson, Richard McElreach, and Oleg Smirnov. 2007. "Egalitarian Motives in Humans." *Nature* 446:794–96.

Diamond, Alexis, and Jasjeet Sekhon. 2007. "Genetic Matching for Estimating Causal Effects." Working paper. http://sekhon.polisci.berkeley.edu/matching/.

Djupe, Paul A., and Anand E. Sokhey. 2011. "Interpersonal Networks and Democratic Politics." *PS: Political Science and Politics* 44 (1):55–59.

Dobson, Douglas, and Duane Meeter. 1974. "Alternative Markov Models for Describing Change in Party Identification." *American Journal of Political Science* 18 (3): 487–500.

Dobson, Douglas, and Douglas St. Angelo. 1975. "Party Identification and the Floating Vote: Some Dynamics." *American Political Science Review* 69 (2): 481–90.

Downs, Anthony. 1957. *An Economic Theory of Democracy*. New York: Harper.

Dreyer, Edward. 1983. "Change and Stability in Party Identification." *Journal of Politics* 35: 712–22.

Druckman, Jamie, Lawrence R. Jacobs, and Eric Ostermeier. 2004. "Candidate Strategies to Prime Issues and Image." *Journal of Politics* 66: 1205–27.

Duflo, Ester, and Emmanuel Saez. 2003. "The Role of Information and Social Interactions in Retirement Plan Decisions: Evidence from a Randomized Experiment." *Quarterly Journal of Economics* 118 (3): 815–42.

Durlauf, Steven N., and Lawrence E. Blume, eds. 2010. "*New Palgrave Dictionary of Economics*, 2nd ed. 8 vols. London: Macmillan.

Eliasoph, Nina. 1998. *Avoiding Politics: How Americans Produce Apathy in Everyday Life*. Cambridge: Cambridge University Press.

Eulau, Heinz. 1963. *The Behavioral Persuasion in Politics*. New York: Random House.

———. 1980. "The Columbia Studies of Personal Influence: Social Network Analysis." *Social Science History* 4 (2): 207–28.

Feddersen, Tim, Sean Gailmard, and Alvaro Sandroni. 2009. "Moral Bias in Large Elections: Theory and Experimental Evidence." *American Political Science Review* 103 (2): 175–92.

Feddersen, Tim, and Alvaro Sandroni. 2009. "The Foundations of Warm-Glow Theory." Working paper.

Feldman, Stanley. 1988. "Structure and Consistency in Public Opinion: The Role of Core Beliefs and Values." *American Journal of Political Science* 32 (2): 416–40.

Festinger, Leon. 1954. "A Theory of Social Comparison Processes." *Human Relations* 7 (2): 117–40.

Fiorina, Morris P. 1981. *Retrospective Voting in American National Elections*. New Haven, CT: Yale University Press.

Fiorina, Morris P., with Samuel J. Abrams and Jeremy C. Pope. 2005. *Culture War? The Myth of a Polarized America*. New York: Pearson Longman.

Fowler, James H. 2005a. "Altruistic Punishment and the Origin of Cooperation." *Proceedings of the National Academy of Sciences* 102 (19): 7047–49.

———. 2005b. "Turnout in a Small World." In *The Social Logic of Politics: Personal Networks as Contexts for Political Behavior*, edited by Alan Zucherman, 269–87. Philadelphia: Temple University Press.

———. 2006a. "Altruism and Turnout." *Journal of Politics* 68 (3): 674–83.

———. 2006b. "Legislative Cosponsorship Networks in the U.S. House and Senate." *Social Networks* 28 (4): 454–65.

Fowler, James H., and Nicholas A. Christakis. 2008a. "Dynamic Spread of Happiness in a Large Social Network: Longitudinal Analysis over 20 Years in the Framingham Heart Study." *British Medical Journal* 337:A2338.

———. 2008b. "Estimating Peer Effects on Health in Social Networks." *Journal of Health Economics* 27 (5): 1400–1405.

Fowler, James H., Tim Johnson, and Oleg Smirnov. 2005. "Egalitarian Motive and Altruistic Punishment." *Nature* 433:E1.

Francia, Peter L., John C. Green, Paul S. Herrnson, Lynda W. Powell, and Clyde Wilcox. 2003. *The Financiers of Congressional Elections: Investors, Ideologues, and Intimates.* New York: Columbia University Press.

Franklin, Charles H. 1984. "Issue Preferences, Socialization, and the Evolution of Party Identification." *American Journal of Political Science* 28 (3): 459–78.

Franklin, Charles H., and John E. Jackson. 1983. "The Dynamics of Party Identification." *American Political Science Review* 77 (4): 957–73.

Freeman, L. C. 1977. "A Set of Measures of Centrality Based on Betweenness." *Sociometry* 40:35–41.

———. 1979. "Centrality in Social Networks: Conceptual Clarification." *Social Networks* 1 (3): 215–39.

Freeman, Richard B. 1997. "Working for Nothing: The Supply of Volunteer Labor." *Journal of Labor Economics* 15 (1): 140–66.

Frey, Bruno S., and Stephan Meier. 2004. "Social Comparisons and Pro-Social Behavior: Testing 'Conditional Cooperation' in a Field Experiment." *American Economic Review* 94 (5): 1717–22.

Funk, Carolyn L. 1999. "Bringing the Candidate into Models of Candidate Evaluation." *Journal of Politics* 61 (3): 700–720.

Garcia, Armando, and Bill Pitkin. 2007. "Zip Code Data Book for Los Angeles County Service Planning Area Six South." Report produced by the United Way of Greater Los Angeles.

Garfinkel, Harold. 1984. *Studies in Ethnomethodology.* Malden, MA: Blackwell.

Gerber, Alan, and Donald P. Green. 1998. "Rational Learning and Partisan Attitudes." *American Journal of Political Science* 42 (3): 794–818.

———. 2000. "The Effects of Canvassing, Telephone Calls, and Direct Mail on Voter Turnout: A Field Experiment." *American Political Science Review* 94 (3): 653–63.

———. 2001. "Do Phone Calls Increase Turnout? A Field Experiment." *Public Opinion Quarterly* 65 (1): 75–85.

Gerber, Alan S., Donald P. Green, and Christopher W. Larimer. 2008. "Social Pressure and Voter Turnout: Evidence from a Large-Scale Field Experiment." *American Political Science Review* 102 (1): 33–48.

———. 2010. "An Experiment Testing the Relative Effectiveness of Encouraging Voter Participation by Inducing Feelings of Pride or Shame." *Political Behavior* 32 (3): 409–22.

Gerber, Alan S., Donald P. Green, and Ron Shachar. 2003. "Voting May Be Habit Forming: Evidence from a Randomized Field Experiment." *American Journal of Political Science* 47 (3): 540–50.

Gerlach, Luther, and Virginia Hine. 1970. *People, Power, and Change: Movements of Social Transformation.* Indianapolis: Bobbs-Merrill.

Gierzynski, Anthony. 2000. *Money Rules: Financing Elections in America.* Boulder, CO: Westview.

Gilens, Martin. 2005. "Inequality and Democratic Responsiveness." *Public Opinion Quarterly* 69 (5): 778–96.

Gimpel, James G., Frances E. Lee, and Joshua Kaminski. 2006. "The Geography of Campaign Contributions in American Politics." *Journal of Politics* 68 (3): 626–39.

Gimpel, James G., Frances E. Lee, and Shanna Pearson-Merkowitz. 2008. "The Check Is in the Mail: Interdistrict Funding Flows in Congressional Elections." *American Journal of Political Science* 52 (2): 373–94.

Glazer, Amihai, and Kai Konrad. 1996. "A Signaling Explanation for Charity." *American Economic Review* 86 (4): 1019–28.

Goeree, Jacob K., Margaret A. McConnell, Tiffany Mitchell, Tracey Tromp, and Leeat Yariv. 2010. "The 1/d Law of Giving." *American Economic Journal: Microeconomics,* 2 (1): 183–203.

Goldbert, Arthur S. 1966. "Discerning a Causal Pattern among Data on Voting Behavior." *American Political Science Review* 60 (4): 913–22.

Goldenberg, Suzanne. 2008. "Iraq War My Biggest Regret, Bush Admits." *Guardian,* December 2.

Goren, Paul. 2005. "Party Identification and Core Political Values." *American Journal of Political Science* 49 (4): 882–97.

Gould, Jay M. 1986. *Quality of Life in American Neighborhoods: Levels of Affluence, Toxic Waste, and Cancer Mortality in Residential Zip Code Areas.* Edited by Alice Tepper Marlin. Boulder, CO: Westview.

Granovetter, Mark S. 1973. "The Strength of Weak Ties." *American Journal of Sociology* 78 (6):1360–80.

Grant, J. Tobin, and Thomas J. Rudolph. 2002. "To Give or Not to Give: Modeling Individuals' Contribution Decisions." *Political Behavior* 24 (1): 31–54.

Green, Donald P., and Alan S. Gerber. 2008. *Get Out the Vote! How to Increase Voter Turnout.* 2nd ed. Washington, DC: Brookings Institution Press.

Green, Donald P., Alan S. Gerber, and David Nickerson. 2003. "Getting Out the Vote in Local Elections: Results from Six Door-to-Door Canvassing Experiments." *Journal of Politics* 65 (4):1083–96.

Green, Donald P., and Bradley Palmquist. 1990. "Of Artifacts and Partisan Instability." *American Journal of Political Science* 34 (3):872–902.

Green, Donald P., Bradley Palmquist, and Eric Schickler. 2002. *Partisan Hearts and Minds: Political Parties and the Social Identities of Voters.* New Haven, CT: Yale University Press.

Green, Donald P., and Ron Shachar. 2000. "Habit Formation and Political Behavior: Evidence of Consuetude in Voter Turnout." *British Journal of Political Science* 30 (4): 561–73.

Green, Donald P., and Ian Shapiro. 1994. *Pathologies of Rational Choice Theory: A Critique of Applications in Political Science.* New Haven, CT: Yale University Press.

Green, Joshua. 2008. "The Amazing Money Machine: How Silicon Valley

Made Barack Obama This Year's Hottest Start-Up." *Atlantic.* http://www
.theatlantic.com/magazine/archive/2008/06/the-amazing-money-machine/
6809/.

Grose, Christian R., and Carrie A. Russell. 2008. "Avoiding the Vote: A Theory
and Field Experiment of the Social Costs of Public Political Participation."
SSRN Manuscript 1310868.

Grubesic, Tony H. 2008. "Zip Codes and Spatial Analysis: Problems and Prospects." *Socio-Economic Planning Sciences* 42 (2): 129–49.

Grubesic, Tony H., and Timothy C. Matisziw. 2006. "On the Use of Zip Codes
and Zip Code Tabulation Areas (ZCTAs) for the Spatial Analysis of Epi-
demiological Data." *International Journal of Health Geographics* 5 (58),
http://www.ncbi.nlm.nih.gov/pmc/articles/PMC1762013/.

Hamilton, David. 1981. "Cognitive Representation of Persons." In *Social
Cognition*, edited by E. Tory Higgins, C. Peter Herman, and Mark Zanna.
Hillsdale, NJ: Erlbaum Associates.

Harbaugh, W. T. 1996. "If People Vote Because They Like to, Then Why Do So
Many of Them Lie?" *Public Choice* 89 (October): 63–76.

———. 1998. "What Do Donations Buy? A Model of Philanthropy Based on
Prestige and Warm Glow." *Journal of Public Economics* 67 (2): 269–84.

Harmon-Jones, Eddie, Jeff Greenberg, Sheldon Solomon, and Linda Simon.
1996. "The Effects of Mortality Salience on Intergroup Bias between Mini-
mal Groups." *European Journal of Social Psychology* 25: 781–85.

Havenstein, Heather. 2008. "My.Barack.Obama.com Social Network Stays
Online after Election." *Computerworld: Networking and Internet*, November 10.

Higgins, E. Tory, and Gillian King. 1981. "Accessibility of Social Constructs:
Information Processing Consequences of Individual and Contextual Vari-
ability." In *Personality, Cognition, and Social Interaction*, edited by Nancy
Cantor and John Kihlstrom, 71–72. Hillsdale, NJ: Erlbaum Associates.

Ho, Daniel E., Kosuke Imai, Gary King, and Elizabeth A. Stuart. 2007a.
"Matching as Nonparametric Preprocessing for Reducing Model Depen-
dence in Parametric Causal Inference." *Political Analysis* 15 (3):199–36.

———. 2007b. "MatchIt: Nonparametric Preprocessing for Parametric Causal
Inference." http://gking.harvard.edu/matchit.

Honaker, James, Gary King, and Matthew Blackwell. 2001. "Amelia II: A Program for Missing Data." http://gking.harvard.edu/amelia.

Hoxby, Caroline. 2000. "Peer Effects in the Classroom: Learning from Gender
and Race Variation." NBER Working Paper 2867.

Huckfeldt, R. Robert. 1979. "Political Participation and the Neighborhood
Social Context." *American Journal of Political Science* 23 (3): 579–92.

———. 2001. "The Social Communication of Political Expertise." *American
Journal of Political Science* 45 (2): 425–38.

———. 2007. "Information, Persuasion, and Political Communication
Networks." In *Oxford Handbook of Political Behavior*, edited by Rus-
sell J. Dalton and Hans-Dieter Klingemann. Oxford: Oxford University
Press.

Huckfeldt, R. Robert, Paul Allen Beck, Russell J. Dalton, and Jeffrey Levine.

1995. "Political Environment, Cohesive Social Groups, and the Communication of Public Opinion." *American Journal of Political Science* 39 (4): 1025–54.

Huckfeldt, R. Robert, Paul Allen Beck, Russell J. Dalton, Jeffrey Levine, and William Morgan. 1998. "Ambiguity, Distorted Messages, and Nested Environmental Effects on Political Communication." *Journal of Politics* 60 (4): 996–1040.

Huckfeldt, R. Robert, Paul E. Johnson, and John Sprague. 2004. *Political Disagreement: The Survival of Diverse Opinions within Communication Networks.* Cambridge: Cambridge University Press.

Huckfeldt, R. Robert, Jeffrey Levine, William Morgan, and John Sprague. 1998. "Election Campaigns, Social Communication, and the Accessibility of Perceived Discussant Preference." *Political Behavior* 20 (4): 263–94.

Huckfeldt, R. Robert, Eric Plutzer, and John Sprague. 1993. "Alternative Contexts of Political Behavior: Churches, Neighborhoods, and Individuals." *Journal of Politics* 55 (2): 365–81.

Huckfeldt, R. Robert, and John Sprague. 1987. "Networks in Context: The Social Flow of Political Information." *American Political Science Review* 81 (4): 1197–1216.

———. 1988. "Choice, Social Structure, and Political Information: The Information Coercion of Minorities." *American Journal of Political Science* 32 (2): 467–82.

———. 1991. "Discussant Effects on Vote Choice: Intimacy, Structure, and Interdependence." *Journal of Politics* 53 (1): 122–58.

———. 1992. "Political Parties and Electoral Mobilization: Political Structure, Social Structure and the Party Canvass." *American Political Science Review* 86 (1): 70–86.

———. 1995. *Citizens, Politics, and Social Communication: Information and Influence in an Election Campaign.* New York: Cambridge University Press.

Huckfeldt, R. Robert, John Sprague, and Jeffrey Levine. 2000. "The Dynamics of Collective Deliberation in the 1996 Election: Campaign Effects on Accessibility, Certainty, and Accuracy." *American Political Science Review* 94 (3): 641–51.

Ikeda, Ken'ichi, and R. Robert Huckfeldt. 2001. "Political Communication and Disagreement among Citizens in Japan and the United States." *Political Behavior* 23 (1): 23–52.

Imai, Kosuke, Gary King, and Olivia Lau. 2006. "Zelig: Everyone's Statistical Software." http://gking.harvard.edu/zelig.

Isenstadt, Alex. 2009. "Republicans' Outlook Remains Bleak." *Chicago Tribune*, May 2.

Iyengar, Shanto. 1976. "Childhood Learning of Partisanship in a New Nation: The Case of Andhra Pradesh." *American Journal of Political Science* 20 (3): 407–23.

Jackman, Simon, and Lynn Vavreck. 2008. "Constructing the 2007–2008 Cooperative Campaign Analysis Project Sample." Appendix to Cooperative Campaign Analysis Project Codebook. http://web.me.com/vavreck/Lynn_Vavreck/CCAP__files/standaloneAPPENDIX.pdf.

Jackson, John. 1975. "Issues, Party Choices, and Presidential Votes." *American Journal of Political Science* 19 (2): 161–85.

Jackson, Matthew O., and Brian W. Rogers. 2007. "Meeting Strangers and Friends of Friends: How Random Are Social Networks?" *American Economic Review* 97 (3): 890–915.

Jacobson, Gary C. 1980. *Money in Congressional Elections.* New Haven, CT: Yale University Press.

Jennings, M. Kent, and Gregory B. Markus. 1984. "Partisan Orientations over the Long Haul: Results from the Three-Wave Political Socialization Panel Study." *American Political Science Review* 78 (4): 1000–1018.

Jennings, M. Kent, and Richard G. Niemi. 1968. "The Transmission of Political Values from Parent to Child." *American Journal of Political Science* 62:169–84.

———. 1974. *The Political Character of Adolescence: The Influence of Family and Schools.* Princeton, NJ: Princeton University Press.

———. 1981. *Generations and Politics: A Panel Study of Young Adults and Their Parents.* Princeton, NJ: Princeton University Press.

Jones, Ruth S., and Anne H. Hopkins. 1985. "State Campaign Fund Raising: Targets and Response." *Journal of Politics* 47 (2): 427–49.

Karlan, Dean, and Margaret A. McConnell. 2009. "Hey Look at Me: The Effect of Giving Circles on Giving." California Institute of Technology working paper.

Karp, Jeffrey A., and David Brockington. 2005. "Social Desirability and Response Validity: A Comparative Analysis of Overreporting Voter Turnout in Five Countries." *Journal of Politics* 67 (3): 825–40.

Kartik, Navin, and R. Preston McAfee. 2006. "Signaling Character in Electoral Competition." California Institute of Technology working paper. http://ssrn.com/abstract=873404.

Katz, Elihu, and Paul F. Lazarsfeld. 1955. *Personal Influence: The Part Played by People in the Flow of Mass Communications.* New York: Free Press.

Kau, James B., Donald Keenan, and Paul H. Rubin. 1982. "A General Equilibrium Model of Congressional Voting." *Quarterly Journal of Economics* 97 (2): 271–93.

Keith, Bruce E., et al. 1986. "The Partisan Affinities of Independent Leaners." *British Journal of Political Science* 16 (2): 155–85.

———. 1992. *The Myth of the Independent Voter.* Berkeley: University of California Press.

Kenny, C. B. 1992. "Political Participation and Effects from the Social Environment." *American Journal of Political Science* 36 (1): 259–67.

Key, V. O., Jr., and Milton C. Cummings. 1966. *The Responsible Electorate: Rationality in Presidential Voting.* Cambridge, MA: Belknap.

Killworth, Peter D., Eugene C. Johnsen, H. Bernard Russell, Gene A. Shelley, and Christopher McCarty. 1990. "Estimating the Size of Personal Networks." *Social Networks* 12:289–312.

Kinder, Donald R. 1978. "Political Person Perception: The Asymmetrical Influence of Sentiment and Choice on Perceptions of Presidential Candidates." *Journal of Personality and Social Psychology* 36 (8): 859–71.

Kinder, Donald R., and David O. Sears. 1985. "Public Opinion and Political Action." In *Handbook of Social Psychology*, edited by Gardner Lindzey and Elliot Aronson, 659–741. New York: Random House.

King, Gary, James Honaker, Anne Joseph, and Kenneth Scheve. 2001. "Analyzing Incomplete Political Science Data: An Alternative Algorithm for Multiple Imputation." *American Political Science Review* 95 (1): 49–69.

Klofstad, Casey A. 2007. "Talk Leads to Recruitment: How Discussions about Politics and Current Events Increase Civic Participation." *Political Research Quarterly* 60 (2): 180–91.

Klofstad, Casey A., Scott McClurg, and Meredith Rolfe. 2009. "Measurement of Political Discussion Networks: A Comparison of Two 'Name Generator' Procedures." *Public Opinion Quarterly* 73 (3): 462–83.

Knoke, David. 1990. "Networks of Political Action: Toward Theory Construction." *Social Forces* 68 (4): 1041–63.

Knoke, David, and Michael Hout. 1974. "Social and Demographic Factors in American Political Party Affiliation, 1952–72." *American Sociological Review* 39:700–713.

Ku, Leighton, Freya L. Sonenstein, and Joseph H. Pleck. 1993. "Neighborhood, Family, and Work: Influences on the Premarital Behaviors of Adolescent Males." *Social Forces* 72 (2): 479–503.

Lake, R. L., and R. Robert Huckfeldt. 1998. "Social Capital, Social Networks, and Political Participation." *Political Psychology* 19 (3): 567–84.

Larimer, Christopher W. 2009. "Does Election Type Have an Impact on the Effectiveness of Social Pressure Appeals to Voting? Evidence from a Field Experiment." Paper presented at the Annual Meeting of the Midwest Political Science Association, Chicago, IL, April 2–5.

Lau, Richard R., and David P. Redlawsk. 1997. "Voting Correctly." *American Political Science Review* 91 (3): 585–98.

Lazarsfeld, Paul F., Bernard Berelson, and Hazel Gaudet. 1948. *The People's Choice: How the Voter Makes Up His Mind in a Presidential Campaign.* 2nd ed. New York: Columbia University Press.

Lazarsfeld, Paul F., and R. K. Merton. 1954. "Friendship as a Social Process: A Substantive and Methodological Analysis." In *Freedom and Control in Modern Society*, edited by Morroe Berger, Theodore Abel, and Charles H. Page, 18–66. New York: Van Nostrand.

Lazer, David, Brian Rubineau, Carol Chetkovich, Nancy Katz, and Michael A. Neblo. 2008. "Networks and Political Attitudes: Structure, Influence, and Co-Evolution." HKS Faculty Research Working Paper RWP08-044.

Leighley, Jan E. 1990. "Social Interaction and Contextual Influences on Political Participation." *American Politics Quarterly* 18 (4): 459–75.

Lerner, Jennifer S., and Philip E. Tetlock. 1999. "Accounting for the Effects of Accountability." *Psychological Bulletin* 125: 255–75.

Levine, David K., and Thomas R. Palfrey. 2007. "The Paradox of Voter Participation? A Laboratory Study." *American Political Science Review* 101 (1): 143–58.

Levine, J. M. 1989. "Reaction to Opinion Deviance in Small Groups." In

Psychology of Group Influence, 2nd ed., edited by Paul B. Paulus, 187–231. Hillsdale, NJ: Erlbaum.

Levitt, Steve. 1994. "Using Repeat Challengers to Estimate the Effects of Campaign Spending on Election Outcomes in the U.S. House." *Journal of Political Economy*, 102 (4): 777–98.

Liedka, Raymond V. 1991. "Who Do You Know in the Group? Location of Organizations in Interpersonal Networks." *Social Forces* 70 (2): 455–74.

Linardi, Sera, and Margaret Anne McConnell. 2009. "No Excuses for Good Behavior: Volunteering and the Social Environment." *Journal of Public Economics* 95 (5–6): 445–54.

Lipset, Seymour Martin. 1960. *Political Man: The Social Bases of Politics.* Doubleday.

Lupia, Arthur, and Mathew D. McCubbins. 1998. *The Democratic Dilemma: Can Citizens Learn What They Need to Know?* New York: Cambridge University Press.

MacKuen, Michael B. 1990. "Speaking of Politics: Individual Conversational Choice, Public Opinion, and the Prospects for Deliberative Democracy." In *Information and Democratic Processes*, edited by John A. Ferejohn and James H. Kuklinski, 59–99. Urbana: University of Illinois Press.

Mann, Christopher B. 2010. "Is There Backlash to Social Pressure? A Large-Scale Field Experiment on Voter Mobilization." *Political Behavior* 32 (3): 387–407.

Mansbridge, Jane. 2003. "Rethinking Representation." *American Political Science Review* 97 (4): 515–28.

Manski, Charles F. 1993. "Identification of Endogenous Social Effects: The Reflection Problem." *Review of Economic Studies* 60 (3): 531–42.

Maponics. 2010. "Zip Code Maps—Frequently Asked Questions." http://www.maponics.com/products/gis-map-data/zip-code-boundaries/faqs/.

Markus, G. B., and P. Converse. 1979. "A Dynamic Simultaneous Equation Model of Electoral Choice." *American Political Science Review* 73 (4):1055–70.

Marsden, Peter V. 1987. "Core Discussion Networks of Americans." *American Sociological Review* 52 (1): 122–31.

———. 1990. "Network Data and Measurement." *Annual Review of Sociology* 16:435–63.

Martinez, Michael D., and Michael M. Gant. 1990. "Partisan Issue Preferences and Partisan Change." *Political Behavior* 12 (3): 243–64.

McAdam, Doug. 1986. "Recruitment to High-Risk Activism: The Case of Freedom Summer." *American Journal of Sociology* 92 (1): 64–90.

McAdam, Doug, and Ronnelle Paulsen. 1993. "Specifying the Relationship between Social Ties and Activism." *American Journal of Sociology* 99 (3): 640–67.

McCarty, Christopher, Peter D. Killworth, H. Russell Bernard, Eugene C. Johnsen, and Gene A. Shelley. 2001. "Comparing Two Methods for Estimating Network Size." *Human Organization* 60 (1): 28–39.

McClurg, Scott D. 2003. "Social Networks and Political Participation: The

Role of Social Interaction in Explaining Political Participation." *Political Research Quarterly* 56 (4): 449–64.

———. 2006a. "The Electoral Relevance of Political Talk: Examining the Effect of Disagreement and Expertise in Social Networks on Political Participation." *American Journal of Political Science* 50 (3): 737–54.

———. 2006b. "Political Disagreement in Context: The Conditional Effect of Neighborhood Context, Discussion, and Disagreement on Electoral Participation." *Political Behavior* 28 (4): 349–66.

McKelvey, Richard D., and Peter Ordeshook. 1985a. "Elections with Limited Information: A Fulfilled Expectations Model Using Contemporaneous Poll and Endorsement Data as Information Sources." *Journal of Economic Theory* 36:55–85.

———. 1985b. "Sequential Elections with Limited Information." *American Journal of Political Science* 29 (3): 480–512.

———. 1990. "Information and Elections: Retrospective Voting and Rational Expectations." In *Information and the Democratic Processes*, edited by John A. Ferejohn and James H. Kuklinski, 333–62. Urbana: University of Illinois Press.

McKinley, Jesse. 2010. "Whooping Cough Kills 5 in California." *New York Times*, June 23.

McPherson, Miller, Lynn Smith-Lovin, and James M. Cook. 2001. "Birds of a Feather: Homophily in Social Networks." *Annual Review of Sociology* 27:415–44.

Meier, Kenneth J. 1975. "Party Identification and Vote Choice: The Causal Relationship." *Western Political Quarterly* 28 (3):496–505.

Mendelberg, Tali. 2002. "The Deliberative Citizen: Theory and Evidence." In *Political Decision-Making, Deliberation and Participation: Research in Micropolitics*, vol. 6, edited by Michael Delli Carpini, Leonie Huddy, and Robert Y. Shapiro, 151–93.. Greenwich, CT: JAI.

Merei, Ferenc. 1952. "Group Leadership and Institutionalization." In *Readings in Social Psychology*, edited by Guy E. Swanson, Theodore M. Newcomb, and Eugene L. Hartley. New York: Holt.

Michelson, Melissa R., Lisa García Bedolla, and Margaret Anne McConnell. 2009. "Heeding the Call: The Effect of Targeted Two-Round Phone Banks on Voter Turnout." *Journal of Politics* 71 (4): 1549–63.

Milgram, Stanley. 1967. "The Small World Problem." *Psychology Today* 2, 1 (1): 61–67.

Miller, Arthur, Warren Miller, Alden Raine, and Thad Brown. 1976. "A Majority Party in Disarray: Policy Polarization in the 1972 Election." *American Political Science Review* 70: 753–78.

Miller, Warren E., and J. Merrill Shanks. 1996. *The New American Voter*. Cambridge, MA: Harvard University Press.

Mobius, Markus, Paul Niehaus, and Tanya S. Rosenblat. 2005. "Social Learning and Consumer Demand." Working paper. http://trosenblat.web .wesleyan.edu/home.

Mollenhorst, Gerald, Beate Volker, and Henk Flap. 2007. "Social Contexts and Personal Relationships." *Social Networks* 30 (1): 60–68.

————. 2008. "Social Contexts and Core Discussion Networks." *Social Forces* 86 (3): 937–65.

Munshi, Kaivan. 2004. "Social Learning in a Heterogeneous Population: Technology Diffusion in the Indian Green Revolution." *Journal of Development Economics* 73 (1): 185–213.

Mutz, Diana C. 2002a. "The Consequences of Cross-Cutting Networks for Political Participation." *American Journal of Political Science* 46 (4): 838–55.

————. 2002b. "Cross-Cutting Social Networks: Testing Democratic Theory in Practice." *American Political Science Review* 96 (1): 111–26.

————. 2006. *Hearing the Other Side: Deliberative versus Participatory Democracy.* Cambridge: Cambridge University Press.

Mutz, Diana C., and Paul S. Martin. 2001. "Facilitating Communication across Lines of Political Difference: The Role of Mass Media." *American Political Science Review* 95 (1): 97–114.

National Atlas of the United States. 2011. http://nationalatlas.gov/.

Newcomb, Theodore M. 1943. *Personality and Social Change: Attitude Formation in a Student Community.* New York: Dryden.

Newman, Mark E. J. 2001. "Scientific Collaboration Networks: I. Network Construction and Fundamental Results." *Physical Review E* 64:016131–8.

Nickerson, David W. 2008. "Is Voting Contagious? Evidence from Two Field Experiments." *American Political Science Review* 102 (1): 49–57.

Niemi, Richard, Richard Katz, and Donald Newman. 1980. "Reconstructing Past Partisanship: The Failure of the Party Identification Recall Questions." *American Journal of Political Science* 24 (1): 633–51.

Nisbett, Richard E., and Timothy Decamp Wilson. 1977. "Telling More Than We Can Know: Verbal Reports on Mental Processes." *Psychological Review* 84 (3): 231–59.

Oliver, Pamela E., and Gerald Marwell. 1988. "The Paradox of Group Size in Collective Action: A Theory of the Critical Mass. II." *American Sociological Review* 53 (1): 1–8.

Olson, Mancur. 1965. *The Logic of Collective Action: Public Goods and the Theory of Groups.* Cambridge, MA: Harvard University Press.

Padgett, John F. 1993. "Robust Action and the Rise of the Medici, 1400–1434." *American Journal of Sociology* 98 (6): 1259–1319.

Page, Benjamin I., and Calvin C. Jones. 1979. "Reciprocal Effects of Policy Preferences, Party Loyalties and the Vote." *American Political Science Review* 73 (4): 1071–89.

Palfrey, Thomas, and Keith Poole. 1987. "The Relationship between Information, Ideology and Voting Behavior." *American Journal of Political Science* 31 (3): 511–30.

Panagopoulos, Costas. 2009. "Thank You for Voting: Gratitude Expression and Voter Mobilization." Paper presented at the Annual Meeting of the Midwest Political Science Association, Chicago, IL, April.

————. 2010. "Emotions, Motivation and Prosocial Behavior: Field Experimental Tests of Alternative Civic Duty Appeals on Voter Turnout." *Political Behavior* 32 (3): 369–86.

Parker, Amy A., Wayne Staggs, and Gustavo H. Dayan. 2006. "Implications of a 2005 Measles Outbreak in Indiana for Sustained Elimination of Measles in the United States." *New England Journal of Medicine* 355 (5): 447–55.

Plutzer, E. 2002. "Becoming a Habitual Voter: Inertia, Resources, and Growth in Young Adulthood." *American Political Science Review* 96 (1): 41–56.

Porter, Mason A., Peter J. Mucha, M. E. J. Newman, and Casey M. Warmbrand. 2005. "A Network Analysis of Committees in the U.S. House of Representatives." *Proceedings of the National Academy of Sciences of the United States of America* 102 (20):7057–62.

Powell, Lisa M., Sandy Slaterb, Donka Mirtchevaa, Yanjun Baoa, and Frank J. Chaloupkaa. 2007. "Food Store Availability and Neighborhood Characteristics in the United States." *Preventive Medicine* 44 (3): 189–95.

Putnam, Robert D. 1966. "Political Attitudes and the Local Community." *American Political Science Review* 60 (3): 640–54.

———. 2000. *Bowling Alone: The Collapse and Revival of American Community*. New York: Simon and Schuster.

Rao, Neel, Markus Mobius, and Tanya S. Rosenblat. 2006. "Social Networks and Vaccination Decisions." Working paper. http://trosenblat.web.wesleyan.edu/home.

Rawls, John. 1993. *Political Liberalism*. New York: Columbia University Press.

Riker, William H., and Peter C. Ordeshook. 1968. "A Theory of the Calculus of Voting." *American Political Science Review* 62 (1): 25–42.

Rolfe, Meredith. 2012. *Voter Turnout: A Social Theory of Political Participation*. Cambridge: Cambridge University Press.

Rosenbaum, Paul R. 2002. *Observational Studies*. 2nd ed. New York: Springer-Verlag.

Rosenbaum, Paul R., and Donald Rubin. 1983. "The Central Role of the Propensity Score in Observational Studies for Causal Effects." *Biometrika* 70:41–55.

———. 1984. "Reducing Bias in Observational Studies Using Subclassification on the Propensity Score." *Journal of the American Statistical Association* 79 (387): 516–24.

Rosenstone, Steven J., and John Mark Hansen. 1993. *Mobilization, Participation, and Democracy in America*. New York: Macmillan, 1993.

Ross, Lee, Gunter Bierbrauer, and Susan Hoffman. 1976. "The Role of Attribution Processes in Conformity and Dissent." *American Psychologist* 31:148–57.

Rubin, Donald. 1974. "Estimating Causal Effects of Treatments in Randomized and Nonrandomized Studies." *Journal of Educational Psychology* 66 (5): 688–701.

Scheff, Thomas J. 2000. "Shame and the Social Bond: A Sociological Theory." *American Sociological Association* 18 (1): 84–99.

Schmitt-Beck, Rudiger. 2003. "Mass Communication, Personal Communication and Vote Choice: The Filter Hypothesis of Media Influence in Comparative Perspective." *British Journal of Political Science* 33 (2): 233–59.

Schuessler, Alexander A. 2000. *A Logic of Expressive Choice*. Princeton, NJ: Princeton University Press.

Schultz, P. Wesley. 1999. "Changing Behavior with Normative Feedback Interventions: A Field Experiment of Curbside Recycling." *Basic and Applied Social Psychology* 21:25–36.

Schultz, P. Wesley, Jessica M. Nolan, Robert B. Cialdini, Noah J. Goldstein, and Vladas Griskevicius. 2007. "The Constructive, Destructive, and Reconstructive Power of Social Norms." *Psychological Science* 18 (5): 429–34.

Searing, Donald D., Joel J. Schwartz, and Alden E. Lind. 1973. "The Structuring Principle: Political Socialization and Belief Systems." *American Political Science Review* 67 (2): 415–32.

Sears, David O., and Carolyn L. Funk. 1999. "Evidence of the Long-Term Persistence of Adults' Political Predispositions." *Journal of Politics* 61 (1): 1–28.

Sears, David O., and Nicholas A. Valentino. 1997. "Politics Matters: Political Events as Catalysts for Preadult Socialization." *American Political Science Review* 91 (1): 45–65.

Shalizi, C. R., and A. C. Thomas. 2011. "Homophily and Contagion Are Generically Confounded in Observational Social Network Studies." *Sociological Methods and Research* 40 (2): 211–39.

Shang, Jen, and Rachel Croson. 2006. "Field Experiments in Charitable Contribution: The Impact of Social Influence on the Voluntary Provision of Public Goods." Wharton working paper.

———. 2009. "Field Experiments in Charitable Contribution: The Impact of Social Influence on the Voluntary Provision of Public Goods." *Economic Journal* 119 (540): 1422–39.

———. 2010. "The Impact of Social Comparisons on Nonprofit Fundraising." *Research in Experimental Economics* 11:143–56.

Shang, Jen, Rachel Croson, and Americus Reed II. Forthcoming. "'I' Give, but 'We' Give More: The Impact of Identity and the Mere Social Information Effect on Donation Behavior." *Journal of Marketing Research*.

Sheingold, Carl. 1973. "Social Networks and Voting: The Resurrection of a Research Agenda." *American Sociological Review* 38 (6): 712–20.

Silberman, Jonathan I., and Gary C. Durden. 1976. "Determining Legislative Preferences on the Minimum Approach." *Journal of Political Economy* 84:317–29.

Silver, Brian D., Barbara A. Anderson, and Paul R. Abrahamson. 1986. "Who Overreports Voting?" *American Political Science Review* 80 (2): 613–24.

Sinclair, Betsy. 2010. "Design and Analysis of Experiments in Multi-level Populations." In *Experimental Handbook*, edited by Jamie Druckman, Donald P. Green, and Skip Lupia, 481–93. New York: Cambridge University Press.

Sinclair, Betsy, Margaret Anne McConnell, and Donald P. Green. 2010. "Detecting Social Networks: Design and Analysis of Multi-level Experiments." Paper presented at the Third Annual CESS NYU Experimental Political Science Conference, February 5–6.

Sinclair, Betsy, Margaret Anne McConnell, and Melissa R. Michelson. 2010. "Local Canvassing and Interpersonal Ties: The Efficacy of Grassroots Voter Mobilization." Working paper.

Snyder, James M., Jr. 1990. "Campaign Contributions as Investments: The House of Representatives, 1980–1987." *Journal of Political Economy* 98 (6): 1195–1227.

Sokhey, Anand, and Scott McClurg. 2008. "Social Networks and Correct Voting." Paper presented at the Harvard Conference on Networks in Political Science, Cambridge, MA, June 2008.

Steiner, Ivan D. 1954. "Primary Group Influence on Public Opinion." *American Sociological Review* 19 (3): 260–67.

Stern, Paul C., Thomas Dietz, Troy Abel, Gregory A. Guagnano, and Linda Kalof. 1999. "A Value-Belief-Norm Theory of Support for Social Movements: The Case of Environmental Concern." *Human Ecology Review* 6 (2): 81–97.

Stokes, Donald E. 1962. "Party Loyalty and the Likelihood of Deviating Elections." *Journal of Politics* 24 (4): 689–702.

Straits, Bruce C. 1991. "Bringing Strong Ties Back in Interpersonal Gateways to Political Information and Influence." *Public Opinion Quarterly* 55 (3): 432–48.

Sunstein, Cass. 2001. *Republic.com*. Princeton, NJ: Princeton University Press.

Tempel, Eugene R., ed. 2003. *Hank Rosso's Achieving Excellence in Fundraising*. 2nd ed.. San Francisco: Jossey-Bass.

Timpone, Richard J. 1998. "Structure, Behavior, and Voter Turnout in the United States." *American Political Science Review* 92 (1): 145–58.

Tomz, Michael, Jason Wittenberg, and Gary King. 2001. "Clarify: Software for Interpreting and Presenting Statistical Results." http://www.stanford.edu/~tomz/software/clarify.pdf.

VanderWeele, T. J., and O. A. Arah. 2012. "Bias Formulas for Sensitivity Analysis of Unmeasured Confounding for General Outcomes, Treatments, and Confounders." *Epidemiology* 23 (1):175–76.

Veblen, T. 1899. *The Theory of the Leisure Class*. New York: Penguin.

Verba, Sidney, and Norman H. Nie. 1972. *Participation in America: Political Democracy and Social Equality*. Chicago: University of Chicago Press.

Verba, Sidney, Kay Lehman Schlozman, and Henry E. Brady. 1995. *Voice and Equality: Civic Voluntarism in American Politics*. Cambridge, MA: Harvard University Press.

Vesterlund, L. 2003. "The Informational Value of Sequential Fundraising." *Journal of Public Economics* 87 (3–4): 627–57.

Walsh, Katherine Cramer. 2004. *Talking about Politics: Informal Groups and Social Identity in American Life*. Chicago: University of Chicago Press.

Weatherford, M. Stephen. 1982. "Interpersonal Networks and Political Behavior." *American Journal of Political Science* 26 (1): 117–43.

Wolfinger, Raymond E., and Steven J. Rosenstone. 1980. *Who Votes?* New Haven, CT: Yale University Press.

Yunus, Muhammud. 2003. *Banker to the Poor: Micro-Lending and the Battle against World Poverty*. New York: Public Affairs.

Zaller, John. 1992. *The Nature and Origins of Mass Opinion*. Cambridge: Cambridge University Press.

Zheng, Tian, Matthew J. Salganik, and Andrew Gelman. 2006. "How Many People Do You Know In Prison? Using Overdispersion in Count Data to Estimate Social Structure in Networks." *Journal of the American Statistical Association* 101 (474): 409–23.

Zimmer, Ron W., and Eugenia F. Toma. 1999. "Peer Effects in Private and Public Schools Across Counties." *Journal of Policy Analysis and Management* 19 (1): 75–92.

Index

Made in the USA
San Bernardino, CA
30 May 2013